VF-11/111

'Sundowners' 1942-95

Aviation Elite Units • 36

OSPREY
PUBLISHING

VF-11/111
'Sundowners' 1942-95

Barrett Tillman with Henk van der Lugt
Series editor Tony Holmes

Front Cover
On the afternoon of 12 January 1945, VF-11 Hellcats launched from USS *Hornet* (CV-12) to attack Tan Son Nhut airport, in French Indochina. Armed with 0.50-cal machine guns and 5-inch High-Velocity Aerial Rockets (HVARs), the F6F pilots strafed parked Japanese aircraft and fired their projectiles into buildings and hangars. Leading the second section in Lt James S Swope's division was Lt(jg) H Blake Moranville. Nicknamed 'Rabbit' because of the similarity of his surname to a famous pre-war baseball player, Moranville was a 21-year-old ace with six victories to his credit. During a low-level pass over the target his F6F-5 BuNo 70680, call sign 'Ginger 30', was hit by ground fire. As he pulled off the target Moranville's wingman called 'Hey "Rabbit", you're on fire!'

The fighter's Pratt & Whitney R2800 was leaking oil, which had ignited, although it soon burned out. With his engine gauges showing falling oil pressure and increasing temperature, Moranville knew he had only minutes remaining in the air. He headed southwest away from Tan Son Nhut, flying 75 miles before his engine seized. 'I saw a big rice paddy and decided to belly in there', Moranville recalled. 'I set up a landing pattern and locked my canopy back, tightened my shoulder harness and dropped my tailhook – the latter would tell me when I had gotten down to within a few feet of the water. I kept my flaps up until I'd cleared a row of trees'.

Moranville executed a successful landing and was escorted to temporary safety by friendly villagers. They summoned a Vichy official, who delivered the aviator to Saigon's central prison where American fliers were kept away from the Japanese. Eventually, Moranville's group walked to safety with a French Foreign Legion unit, reaching Dien Bien Phu and being flown to safety in China (*Cover artwork by Mark Postlethwaite*)

First published in Great Britain in 2010 by Osprey Publishing, Midland House, West Way, Botley, Oxford OX2 0PH, UK
44-02 23rd St, Suite 219, Long Island City, NY 11101, USA
E-mail; info@ospreypublishing.com

A CIP catalogue record for this book is available from the British Library

Print ISBN 978 1 84603 484 8
PDF e-book ISBN 978 1 84908 263 1

Edited by Tony Holmes
Page design by Mark Holt
Cover artwork by Mark Postlethwaite
Aircraft Profiles and Unit Insignia by Tom Tullis
Index by Michael Forder
Originated by PQD Digital Media Solutions, Suffolk, UK
Printed and bound in China through Bookbuilders

10 11 12 13 14   10 9 8 7 6 5 4 3 2 1

FOR A CATALOGUE OF ALL BOOKS PUBLISHED BY OSPREY MILITARY AND AVIATION PLEASE CONTACT:

Osprey Direct, c/o Random House Distribution Center,
400 Hahn Road, Westminster, MD 21157
Email: uscustomerservice@ospreypublishing.com

Osprey Direct, The Book Service Ltd, Distribution Centre,
Colchester Road, Frating Green, Colchester, Essex, CO7 7DW
Email: customerservice@ospreypublishing.com

www.ospreypublishing.com

CONTENTS

GUADALCANAL

August 1942 was a noteworthy month in the history of World War 2. In the Mediterranean, U-boats ravaged a British convoy bound for Malta, and the *Afrika Korps* was repulsed at Alam Halfa, ending the First Battle of El Alamein. In Europe, the fledgling Eighth Air Force flew its first missions over Occupied France, while an Anglo-Canadian force launched a large-scale raid against Dieppe. In Moscow, Soviet dictator Josef Stalin and British Prime Minister Winston Churchill – philosophical enemies to the bone – met to plot strategy against Adolf Hitler. Of lasting importance in the Pacific was the 7 August amphibious landing at Guadalcanal, a previously obscure island in the Solomons chain. The 1st Marine Division's tenuous beachhead represented the first US offensive of the war, initiating a six-month bloodletting that would prove crucial in the defeat of Imperial Japan.

That same week a new fighter squadron was being formed at San Diego's North Island Naval Air Station (NAS). Establishing a new unit was nothing unusual at the time, as it was a hectic expansion period for the US Navy. Since the Battle of the Coral Sea in May, America had lost the aircraft carriers USS *Lexington* (CV-2) and USS *Yorktown* (CV-5), putting most of their aviators ashore for reassignment.

North Island's new fighter squadron was designated VF-11, the fourth 'FitRon' established in 1942. However, the unit's date of origin has been erroneously reported for over half a century. For obscure reasons the US Navy still officially lists VF-11's establishment date as 10 October 1942. The latter likely reflects the date that the original replacement air group became a fleet unit – Carrier Air Group (CAG) 11. In any case, the squadron that became the 'Sundowners' definitely existed prior to October. The July report for location of naval aircraft shows CAG-11 'organising at San Diego'. By 27 August the roster was full with 76 aircraft, including 27 fighters, 30 dive-bombers and 19 torpedo-bombers. The earliest known logbook for the original VF-11 cadre shows the squadron generating flights in early August.

'Fighting 11' was the recipient of several displaced pilots, including its commanding officer, Lt Cdr Charles R Fenton. A 35-year-old native of Annapolis, Maryland, Fenton had graduated from the US Naval Academy (USNA) in 1929, ranking 185th of 240. Previously, he was commanding officer of VF-42 aboard *Yorktown*. His flight officer, Lt William N Leonard (USNA 1937), was one of the top-scoring carrier pilots in the first phase of the Pacific War with four confirmed victories and a probable to his credit while flying with VF-42 and VF-3 at the Battles of Coral Sea and Midway.

Two other combat-experienced pilots posted to VF-11 were Lt Frank B Quady (one shared victory) and Lt(jg) Walter J Hiebert, both formerly of VF-6 aboard USS *Enterprise* (CV-6). Quady became VF-11's engineering officer while Hiebert took charge of communications. The remaining three senior pilots had seen no combat, but were experienced fliers. Lt Clarence M White Jr was designated executive officer and Lt Raymond W Vogel (40th of 261 in the USNA Class of 1936) became operations officer. Lt Gordon D Cady ran the gunnery department, and VF-11 was fortunate to have him, as he was developing the boresight gun pattern for the Grumman F4F-4 Wildcat. In addition to being experienced aviators, four of VF-11's six senior pilots were graduates of the USNA. That depth of leadership was unusual.

'Fighting 11' was operating F4F-4s by 11 August, and it slowly began adding new, younger pilots to its ranks. When CAG-11 was established on 10 October under Cdr Paul H Ramsey, Fenton's squadron had about 27 pilots. They included one 'white hat', Chief Aviation Pilot Chester A Parker, who was later commissioned. Future standouts in the squadron were Ens James S Swope, a tall, blond Texan who had earned a private pilot's license before joining the Navy, and Ens Vernon E Graham, a rugged, good-looking Colorado pilot. Ens Charles R Stimpson's nickname was 'Skull' after his thin appearance, but it would prove appropriate for another reason. Lanky and personable, the 23-year-old Utah native joined the squadron with 525 hours in his logbook, and he would become the deadliest of all VF-11 aviators.

After barely two months at North Island, the air group deployed to Hawaii, departing the West Coast on 23 October. Most personnel went by transport ship, but the more experienced fighter pilots, and 13 Wildcats (half the authorised strength), embarked in the escort carrier USS *Chenango* (ACV-28). Upon arrival in Hawaii, the bomber, scout and torpedo squadrons were based at NAS Barbers Point, on Oahu, but VF-11 went to NAS Maui, which was decidedly less crowded.

Fenton began accumulating more aircraft as VF-11 embarked upon a comprehensive training programme that emphasised aerial gunnery and strafing – a number of 'group gropes' with other squadrons in CAG-11

Ens Charles R Stimpson and AMM2c Kermit H Enander pose upon Stimpson's Wildcat on Maui, circa October 1942. Stimpson's aircraft originally received the side number F16, but this was changed to F4 when he joined Lt Cdr White's division upon arriving on Guadalcanal. Enander was the driving force behind the CAG-11 reunion association that ran after the war (*via Tim Enander*)

The von Tempsky estate on Maui became the 'Sundowners'' second home between both combat deployments. The ranching family adopted VF-11 and other squadrons, flying a special flag to indicate that 'buzz jobs' were authorised when dignitaries were absent! (*via Rich Leonard*)

also took place. But it was not all work, for 'Fighting 11' had been adopted by a prosperous Maui couple, Boyd and Maria von Tempsky, who operated a large cattle ranch. The von Tempskys had two sons in Europe with the USAAF, and along with Boyd's sister Alexa, they had become fond of US Navy fighter squadrons. Fenton's pilots quickly came to appreciate 'the civilised chow, sports, music and other reminders of home' that the estate on the upper slopes of Haleakala Mountain afforded.

While on Maui some of the pilots took steps that defined the squadron's heraldry and terminology. Bill Leonard, Charlie Stimpson and one or two others decided that VF-11 should have an insignia, so they devised the concept of two stubby Grummans shooting a 'rising sun' into the ocean as representative of their mission. With the help of Alexa and Maria, the insignia was rendered in colour, and squadron mechanics devised a multiple stencil system so that each Wildcat could have identical emblems. Lt Cdr Fenton approved the idea, and thus was born one of the most enduring insignia in US naval aviation.

Numerals were not allowed on unit emblems but along the bottom was printed *SUN DOWNERS*, though subsequently the name was usually rendered as one word. It referred mainly to the squadron's job of shooting down Japanese 'suns', but that was only part of the story. As Leonard explained, '"Sundowner" was an old nautical appellation that referred to a diligent worker – a sailor who toiled till day was done. It originated in the days of sail when grog was customarily served on ships, but a strict captain might withhold the ration until dark while others relented when the sun sank below the main yardarm'.

'Sundowner' shooters examine a target sleeve after a gunnery flight at Maui. They are, from left to right, Leonard, Vogel, Swope and Gaston (*via Rich Leonard*)

Much later another squadron bore the 'Sundowner' title owing to confusion in the Navy Bureau of Aeronautics (BuAer). 'Fighting 86' formed at Atlantic City, New Jersey, in June 1944 and gained approval for the name that November. The error was not discovered within BuAer until June 1945 when the squadron was deployed in WestPac. At that point VF-86 became the 'Wild Hares' until disestablished five months later.

In Hawaii the pilots averaged 35 or more hours per month – mostly 'red-meat fighter flights' emphasising gunnery and tactics. However, a few like Bill Leonard took the opportunity to log 'familiarisation' flights in P-40s.

'Fighting 11's' training ended in February 1943 when the squadron, filled out with about 35 aircraft and 40 pilots, boarded the escort carriers USS *Long Island* (ACV-1) and USS *Altamaha* (ACV-18) and headed southwest. On 6 March the F4Fs were catapulted off the CVEs' short decks for Nandi, in the Fijian islands. The 'Sundowners' were put on short notice for deployment to Guadalcanal, but at virtually the same time the unit lost its skipper, Charlie Fenton. Recalled for duty in Washington, D.C. after six months as CO, Fenton turned over to his

The 'Sundowners' at Maui on 29 January 1943. These pilots are, front row, from left to right, Wesley, Quady, Cady, C M White, Fenton, Vogel, Leonard and Heibert. In the middle row, from left to right, are Parker, Cooke, H S White, Maxwell, Graham, Swope, Slagle, Graber, Johnson and Gilbert. In the third row, from left to right, are Dayhoff, Ricker, Stimpson, Holberton, Cary, Ogilvie, Ramsey and Flath (*via Tim Enander*)

'Fighting 11's' distinctive insignia was devised in Hawaii prior to the 1943 Guadalcanal deployment. Lt William N Leonard, Ens Charles Stimpson and a few others suggested the 'Sun Downer' name as a pun on their mission of downing Japanese 'suns' and the old nautical term denoting a hard worker. The emblem remained to the end of the squadron's existence in 1995 with little modification (*via Tailhook Association*)

Above right
A 1943 *SUN DOWNERS* patch that was never used. The originals were stencilled on naugahyde, then cut out for sewing onto flight jackets and other garments (*via Rich Leonard*)

executive officer, Charles White, while Raymond 'Sully' Vogel took the 'exec' position. Bill Leonard assumed the combined duties of flight and operations officer.

White and Vogel took different approaches to leadership. White was regarded as 'a stickler for obeying the rules', being especially insistent on radio discipline – 'If not in use, turn off the juice'. Vogel, according to wingman Bob Flath, was 'more laid back in dealing with us red-assed ensigns'.

Training continued at Nandi, covering such esoteric missions as night strafing, both individually and by divisions. Then in late April the squadron obtained drop tanks for the long over-water flight to Espiritu Santo and on to Guadalcanal. The 'drops' worked reasonably well, although Bill Leonard's starboard tank fell off during his initial test hop.

CAG-11 was combat-ready under Lt Cdr Weldon L Hamilton, a veteran of the Coral Sea battle and an inspirational leader. The pilots were qualified for carrier operations, but during the period VF-11 spent at North Island the US Navy had lost three more carriers. Whilst the 'Sundowners' had been getting organised in August and September the early battles around Guadalcanal had seen USS *Saratoga* (CV-3) sent to the dockyard with torpedo damage and USS *Wasp* (CV-7) sunk by a Japanese submarine. Then, just days after the air group left San Diego, USS *Hornet* (CV-8) was lost in the Battle of Santa Cruz. By the time

A close-up view of one of the panels from Lt W N Leonard's Wildcat, showing the original rendering of the 'Sun Downers' emblem (*via Rich Leonard*)

Boys will be boys during squadron high jinks at the von Tempsky estate in early 1943 before Lt Cdr C R Fenton was relieved by C M White. These men are, from left to right, Gaston, Charles Fenton and Hiebert (*via Rich Leonard*)

CAG-11 arrived in the combat zone only *Enterprise* remained in action. Therefore, Hamilton's squadrons would go ashore on Guadalcanal to operate with the US Marine Corps.

It was disappointing to the fighter pilots, who were aware that their F4Fs were outclassed by the faster, more versatile Vought F4U-1 – the Marine fighter squadrons at Guadalcanal would be flying Corsairs by the time VF-11 arrived because the 'U-Bird' was considered unsuitable for carrier operations. The Wildcat was a well-proven aircraft, but now that the 'Sundowners' were to operate from land they would have preferred F4Us. The F4F lacked not only the Corsair's speed, but its range, rate of climb and ammunition capacity.

One advantage was that there would be no shortage of Wildcats. 'Fighting 11' and VF-21 were the last F4F squadrons engaged in prolonged combat, and the Fleet Aircraft Replacement Pool was well stocked with Grummans from other units. As Ens Vern Graham said, 'We were concerned about being selected to "use up" the remaining F4Fs. However, we were confident in the fighter'. Bill Leonard probably summed up the pilots' feelings when he commented, 'Committed to the F4F, we would not let our minds dwell too much on its deficiencies. VF-11 felt sensitive about flying an obviously outdated machine, but we were loyal to the F4F'.

One aviator was completely delighted to fly Wildcats – in fact, Vern Graham was reunited with *his* Wildcat. He wrote, 'I was aching for a fight because I had an aeroplane which I knew from prop to rudder. We had gotten together again after a 12,000-mile journey'. Incredibly, Graham's 'Fox 23' in VF-11 was the same F4F-4 that he

VF-11 flew from the Fijian islands before proceeding to Guadalcanal. During March 1943 the Nandi 'control tower' was operated by Lt C C Flynn, squadron personnel officer, who is being observed here by Frank Quady and Jim Swope. Flynn holds a signal light, providing rudimentary air traffic control (*via Tim Enander*)

had flown in operational training. He had done especially well in BuNo 03430 on gunnery flights, stating, 'Its guns were sweet and I seemed to do better with them than with the guns on any other ship I flew'. But when he left to join his fleet squadron, Graham had never expected to see his 'pet' Grumman again. Nevertheless, half a world away, against all odds, he was reunited with BuNo 03430 and confidently took it into combat.

The pilots' experience level was, if anything, somewhat greater than a mid-war fighting squadron. Bill Leonard landed at Guadalcanal's Cactus Field with 935 hours total time and four confirmed kills. Even some of VF-11's 'young studs' had considerable experience. Charlie Stimpson, for instance, entered combat with more than 800 hours flight time, including 250 in F4Fs.

GUADALCANAL

On 25 April 1943, after six weeks in the Fijian islands, CAG-11 departed for Guadalcanal. White, Cady and Vogel each led one of VF-11's three elements to their destination, with TBFs providing navigation lead on the 600-mile flight. The Wildcats made the 4.5-hour flight to Espiritu Santo that day and logged another 4.3 the next, arriving at 'The Canal' on Monday the 26th with 34 aircraft. Two had been delayed en route with mechanical problems, but both shortly rejoined the squadron. 'Fighting 11' settled down at the Lunga Point strip better known as 'Fighter One', while Cdr Hamilton's other three squadrons were based at nearby Henderson Field.

The ground echelon had previously arrived by ship or transport aeroplane and established a tent camp in what intelligence officer Lt Donald Meyer called 'a delightful oasis of mud and mosquitoes in a coconut grove'. The next day VF-11 was briefed by Col Sam Moore, the colourful, swashbuckling Marine fighter commander. The 'Sundowners' were to fly under the tactical control of the US Marine Corps, as the leathernecks had been operating from the island for the past eight months. Later that morning (the 27th), VF-11's first patrol from 'Cactus' was flown by Lt Cdr Vogel and Lt(jg)s Robert N Flath, William R Maxwell, and Cyrus G Cary. It was a local flight with nothing to report, but two days later Lt Cdr White led two divisions on an escort to Munda. The only enemy opposition was anti-aircraft (AA) fire.

Throughout the combat tour VF-11 was blessed with exceptional maintenance. Prior to any losses, the unit maintained an average 37 of 41 available aircraft fully operational for an initial complement of 38 pilots. The 90 percent readiness rate was partly due to the Wildcat's relative

'Sundowners'' executive officer and skipper pose for a photograph with the squadron 'scoreboards' on Guadalcanal. Lt Raymond W Vogel and Lt Cdr Charles M White are both wearing AN-H pattern cloth helmets and B-7 goggles. Vogel commanded CAG-11 in Korea, where he was killed in action flying an F4U Corsair in August 1950. White died in retirement in 1963 (*via Steve Wells*)

simplicity, but it was also a tribute to Frank Quady's maintenance crew. The 'Sundowners'' mechanics certainly deserved their reputation, as they literally built an extra fighter from the ground up. Using portions of three or four Marine wrecks, the sailors assembled another F4F-4 which they assigned the BuAer number 11!

At the end of the first week (Sunday, 2 May) VF-11 suffered its first loss. Sixteen 'Sundowners' were escorting a strike to Munda when, south of Vangunu, at 14,000 ft the 'exec', Sully Vogel, ran one of his fuel tanks dry and lost altitude while switching tanks. His element leader, Bob Maxwell, moved to port to regain sight of Vogel and the two Wildcats collided. Vogel's propeller sliced off the last six feet of Maxwell's fuselage (BuNo 11757), the F4F nosing up in a half loop and then falling away in a flat spin. Maxwell managed to bail out and opened his parachute, but the other Wildcats had to continue the mission. At 1700 hrs the returning pilots spotted Maxwell in his life raft and reported his position, although it was too late to summon help. Vogel had aborted the mission, returning with a smashed canopy and rubber marks on one wing from Maxwell's tyres.

'Maxie' was nowhere to be seen the next morning, and he remained missing for a full two weeks until a PBY Catalina brought him back to Guadalcanal on 18 May after a harrowing, but safe, 16 days in enemy-occupied territory. The intrepid South Carolinian had sailed his raft to Tetipari, arriving on the 5th. He walked the length of the island in seven days, encountering a crocodile that claimed dominion over a channel on a coral beach, but otherwise Maxwell met no opposition. On the 13th he launched his raft for Rendova, where he knew he might contact an Australian coast watcher. He was met by friendly natives who took him to safety near Segi Lagoon on the 17th.

Maxwell's fifth mission had been his last with VF-11, for he was flown to New Zealand, where he spent the next spent two months in hospital, recuperating from his adventure. Subsequently he joined VF-51, becoming the squadron's only ace aboard USS *San Jacinto* (CVL-30) in 1944.

Lt(jg) Bob Maxwell poses in his assigned Wildcat, coded F20, at Guadalcanal. He was involved in a midair collision on 2 May, bailing out over Tetipari Island and spending two weeks with friendly natives and coastwatchers before being returned to the squadron. Evacuated with injuries, he was reassigned and became an ace flying with VF-51 in 1944 (*via Henk van der Lugt*)

Meanwhile, operations continued, and despite the lack of aerial opposition the losses mounted. On 6 May, during another Munda strike, Ens LeRoy Childs' aircraft (BuNo 11922) dropped behind the formation, its engine smoking badly. The F4F splashed down north of Rendova hook, and although Maxwell talked to natives who saw a parachute that day, only Childs' seat cushion was found.

Two days later three 'Sundowners' led by Lt Lester Wall found enemy shipping in Blackett Strait between Vella Gulf and Kula Gulf. They shot a landing barge to pieces, then found a Japanese ship dead in the water. It was *Oyashio*, a 2400-ton destroyer that had struck a mine the previous night. The Wildcats raked the crippled ship repeatedly, facilitating its eventual sinking five miles southwest of Rendova.

On 26 May the skipper achieved the dubious distinction of being the first VF-11 pilot to qualify for the Purple Heart. A 20 mm shell went through White's cockpit while he strafed Suavanau Point at Rekata Bay, causing a gash on his left hand. He returned to flight status one week later.

Although things were slow in the air, the squadron's living area was improved considerably by the industrious Sea Bees, who built Quonset huts and new shower stalls. Two pilots had been evacuated to New Zealand during the first weeks of the deployment suffering from jaundice, but otherwise the squadron largely enjoyed good health. Dysentery was the most troublesome ailment, but it grounded few pilots, and none for long.

On 6 June the entire air group suffered a heartfelt loss when CAG Weldon Hamilton died in a C-47 crash along with several VT-11 personnel. Hamilton's death was keenly felt, as a bomber pilot in CAG-11 said he 'led every attack and could smell out enemy ships in bad weather. A great man, swell guy – the kind of man that will win this war'. His successor was Lt Cdr Frederick Ashworth of 'Torpedo 11', who would in fact have a hand in winning the war. Three years later he was the weaponeer on the atom bomb that destroyed Nagasaki.

By the first week of June VF-11 had been on Guadalcanal a month-and-a-half without a single claim for an enemy aircraft. The 'Sundowner' appellation was beginning to seem unduly boastful, particularly in comparison to the record of most Marine squadrons in-theatre. Gordon Cady's division finally broke the ice on 7 June when a 32-aeroplane escort to Vila was abandoned due to weather. Cady had led his four fighters up to 10,000 ft and, seeing the route was clear farther west, received permission to continue.

The Wildcats were ten miles south of Segi when an estimated 24 Zero-sens were sighted approaching overhead at 15,000 ft. At the same time Lt(jg) Daniel Hubler – the No 4 man – reported at least eight more directly above. Climbing at 130 knots, outnumbered eight-to-one and at a serious tactical disadvantage, Cady wisely decided to evade into clouds over Vangunu while he could. But it was already too late for the other three. Hubler's aeroplane (BuNo 11871) was so badly shot up that he had to bail out, and typically the Japanese strafed him in the water. Fortunately, all of them missed. Other enemy fighters concentrated on Lt(jg)s Terry Holberton and Ed 'Smiley' Johnson. Holberton recalled the encounter;

'Speculation had been that the Japanese used their machine guns with tracers to boresight the target, then opened up with their 20 mm cannon. Some small shot came through the side of my aircraft, wiping out the circuit breakers and the instrument panel. All electricity went out, including the gunsight. I believe the shots were all from bullets. A larger round hit me in the starboard wing root and took out the oil cooler. One of the smaller rounds ran down my arm from elbow to wrist, burning the skin.

'About that time I hit the cloud cover over Vangunu. I set the gyro compass to zero and made a sharp 90-degree turn to the left, counting slowly to 30 while on instruments. I reset the compass to zero again and turned 180 degrees, counting slowly for 30 seconds, then turned left and came out of the clouds on the original course. There was "Smiley" just ahead of me, chased by a Zero so intent on the kill that he never saw me.

'My windscreen was filled with the Zero so I didn't need sights. He was slightly above me and I pulled up and squeezed the trigger. Nothing happened because the electrical system was out. Then the engine quit due to the strain. I had no oil pressure and the prop was running wild. I pushed over to keep from stalling and headed for the vast lagoon between New Georgia and Vangunu. Dead-sticking the aeroplane (BuNo 11751) into the water, I hit my head on the gunsight, and was knocked unconscious. The next thing I knew I was sitting in the cockpit with water up to my chin.'

Flying as Cady's section leader was Lt(jg) Edward H Johnson, who saw the skipper abruptly break into a right-hand dive. 'Smiley' figured that Cady's initial move was to seek cover in the clouds over Vangunu, but the 'Sundowners' were boxed in as the estimated eight Zero-sens rolled in from overhead. Johnson caught fleeting glimpses of the disaster – Hubler's aeroplane staggering in a stream of tracers, Holberton's under attack by three bandits and Cady taking fire from above. Johnson had his own concern as tracers slashed past him, accompanied by metallic impacts somewhere behind him. There ensued an interminable period stretching past two minutes before he plunged into the cloud.

But it was too late. Johnson's engine cut in and out before he emerged from the thin cloud. On the opposite side two or three more Japanese fighters set upon him, shooting his F4F to shreds. He recalled;

'The cockpit began to get exceedingly hot, and I was almost sure the aeroplane was afire. My left oil cooler had definitely been hit, and I could see oil streaming out of the wing. I'm sure that my engine had been badly hit. At

Lt(jg)s Bob 'Cactus' Flath and Terry Holberton receive their Purple Hearts for wounds sustained at Guadalcanal. The F4F behind them has had roughly painted horizontal bars added to its fuselage star, dating this photograph as having been taken in late 1943. Flath was one of the 'Sundowners' two-tour pilots, also deploying aboard USS *Hornet* (CV-12) in 1944. He scored a confirmed victory and a probable while F6Fs flying from the vessel (*Flath via Enander*)

different times I heard violent explosions, which could have been cylinder heads blowing off or exploding 20 mm cannon shells.'

Chased in and out of the cloud layer, Johnson got off one optimistic snap shot that probably missed. Then, descending to 5000 ft, his much-abused Pratt & Whitney seized up. He nosed down to maintain airspeed, slid the canopy back, unfastened his safety belt (there were no shoulder harnesses yet) and popped the control column forward. Johnson was ejected from the cockpit, striking his right leg as he exited;

'I pulled my ripcord with both hands almost upon leaving the aeroplane, as I figured that I was between 1000 ft and 1500 ft above the side of the mountain. My 'chute opened with an extremely hard jerk, as I had been diving fast when I got out. I heard my aeroplane crash into the mountainside almost immediately.'

Descending toward the trees, Johnson realised that he was engaged in a lopsided race. A Japanese pilot spotted his parachute and turned in for a gunnery run. 'The Zero dove at me, firing just as I dropped below the tree-tops. Fortunately, I dropped into a hole among the trees, which were at least 80 ft high. The 'chute snagged in the higher branches just enough to slow my fall, and I hit the ground without too much of a jolt'. He unfastened his parachute harness and scrambled for cover, watching the Japanese fighters strafe the area for several minutes before departing.

Once convinced that the bloodthirsty Zero-sen pilots had departed, Johnson checked himself over. He had a four-inch gash behind the right knee that was over an inch wide. However, he wanted to get clear of the shoot-down position as quickly as possible, and made tracks into what he reckoned was the New Georgia interior. Johnson believed that he would not need his rubber raft or 'Mae West' so he left them behind, lest they hinder him or draw attention. As he ruefully conceded, 'My advice to a pilot is never leave anything behind, even though it is inconvenient to carry, and does not seem necessary at the time'. He added a recommendation for salvaging the parachute shroud lines, and stressed the need for an accurate map of the area in the backpack. Only later did he realise he was on Vangunu rather than New Georgia. With that, he chambered a round in his 0.45-cal pistol, consulted the compass in his knife handle and headed east. It was the start of a ten-day exercise in survival.

Cady, meanwhile, had reached the clouds unharmed, and dodged from cover to cover en route to base. He was twice presented with opportunities he could not resist, however, and thereby lived up to his formidable gunnery reputation. On both occasions when Cady emerged from a cloud to find Zero-sens before him, he shot them down. Then he raced back to Guadalcanal to help organise rescue efforts. Amazingly, all three downed 'Sundowners' returned safely, Hubler by native canoe the next day.

Bruised as he was, Holberton made for the nearest small island in his raft, dressed his wounds and launched himself again toward the next island. After reaching shore and pulling his raft along the beach and through mangroves, he rested until dawn. Continuing his trek, he narrowly avoided an encounter with a crocodile, thereafter giving the fresh-water mangroves a wide berth, and came ashore near what seemed

Throughout its Guadalcanal tour VF-11 had a consistently high in-commission rate. Typical of the men 'who kept 'em flying' was Terry Fitzpatrick, plane captain of Lt(jg) Robert 'Cac' Flath's F4F-4 (*via Steve Wells*)

an abandoned village. The following morning he heard voices and saw two silhouettes near a shack;

'I waited for a little light and entered the hut with my 0.45 drawn. The two men were natives, one old and one young. The young one dove out a window too quickly for me to shoot.

'I was yelling, "American pilot! American pilot!" but the old man just kept cringing on the floor until I realised that he was looking down the barrel of my automatic and was scared to death. When the gun was lowered he called the young man, who came back. There was a lot of native chatter and sign language, and I sat down to wait with the old man while the boy took off in a canoe.'

No less than a chief returned with several other natives and an interpreter to bear Terry Holberton to another island. During the dangerous open-water trek around New Georgia to Segi, a flight of VF-11 Wildcats spotted the party and a J2F Duck was called in to rescue Holberton.

'Smiley' Johnson had an even more adventurous trek. Thinking he was on New Georgia, he nearly strolled into a Japanese camp. Johnson then spent 12 days in a survival epic both ashore and at sea. On the third day he scrounged enough wood to build a crude raft from a burned-out boat. Then he slowly paddled along the coast, putting ashore each night. He was nearly seen on the second day when two Japanese barges passed nearby. Johnson hid behind his crude raft, knowing that his pistol was rusted into uselessness. Forced inland again, the 'Sundowner' 'borrowed' some mats from a native hut and established a hiding spot. He related, 'My hideout was so well hidden I had trouble getting into it myself.' The next day he continued walking, although the soles of his shoes had by now been scraped thin by the coral.

On 13 June Johnson approached a clearing on his belly, having seen footprints previously. Lurking in the mud, he gawked at ten Japanese soldiers a few yards away. Johnson related, 'One of them was the biggest SOB I ever saw in my life. He must have been about six feet four. Don't ever let anybody tell you the Japs are small, scrawny and ill nourished. These were plenty big and plenty tough looking!'

Following that near miss, Johnson backtracked to his raft and paddled for two more days before locating some friendly natives. Then, with the help of an Australian coast watcher, he made his way to Segi (on the southern tip of New Georgia) and was retrieved by a PBY Catalina. Stepping onto Henderson Field on 19 June, he commented, 'It looked as good as my own front yard in Coronado, except my wife was not there'.

The Johnson saga had a bittersweet ending. He was sent home to recover and rejoined his wife, whereupon he learned that his brother had been killed in Europe. Johnson attended the funeral on the east coast, then caught a ride back west on a USAAF bomber. The aircraft crashed and Johnson – the US Navy hitchhiker – was the only man killed.

Later on 7 June, 'Sully' Vogel led his division to Vila for some strafing, before hedgehopping home via New Georgia and Gatukai. Between Gatukai and the Russells, Lt(jg) Robert Flath was bounced by

Lt(jg) Charles V Wesley with an F4F plane captain. VF-11's Wildcat F13 was assigned to Lt Kenneth T Viall, while Wesley's aircraft nominally was F33 (*via Steve Wells*)

The squadron's operations and flight officer was Lt William N Leonard, seen here on Guadalcanal on 15 June 1943. Leonard possessed more combat experience than any other VF-11 pilot on 'Cactus', having flown with VF-42 from USS *Yorktown* (CV-5) during the Battles of Coral Sea and Midway (*via Rich Leonard*)

two 'Zekes' that badly shot up his aeroplane. Vogel boresighted one Zero-sen and shot it off Flath's tail, allowing his squadronmate to dive for home. Vogel managed to elude the second bandit.

In the aerial encounters of 7 June, VF-11 had come out even at three for three, but lost no pilots. However, it was painfully obvious that the Wildcats could not hope for much better than a draw when outnumbered and caught at a disadvantage.

The next combat came only five days later, with much better results. Four divisions under Bill Leonard were returning from a long PBY escort at 0940 hrs when the fighter director reported a large contact on his radar. Leonard, Lt Kenneth T Viall and Lt(jg)s Les Wall and Charles V Wesley reported their divisions available for interception and spent the next 35 minutes following radar vectors. Visual contact was made shortly after 1000 hrs northwest of the Russells when, stacked from 23,000 ft up to 26,000 ft, the 16 Wildcats saw some three-dozen Zeros-sens both above and below them. Leonard evaluated the situation, mainly concerned about the F4Fs' dwindling fuel, for they had been in the air well over three hours. He radioed, 'Make one pass and use remaining fuel to get home', which was 70 miles away.

As was often the case, going directly home was not possible. Leonard destroyed two 'Zekes', raising his career total to six, then disengaged, but the Japanese pressed their numerical advantage and drew most of the other Wildcats into dogfights. Lt(jg) Claude Ivie splashed a 'Zeke' but was forced to ditch near the Russells, while the other pilots became scattered and fought singly or in pairs.

Leonard's second section did not make it clear of the Zero-sens either. Lt(jg) Vern Graham and his wingman, Lt(jg) Robert L Gilbert, 'became involved in assisting Marine F4Us who were severely outnumbered', as Graham put it. The Corsairs had been drawn to the combat and, with more fuel, stayed to fight. Gilbert remained as long as he dared, claiming three kills, then broke off, rejoined Leonard and landed with less than four gallons of fuel left in his tanks. Lt Ken Viall's division was bounced by several 'Zekes' but he disregarded bandits on his tail and drew a bead on one of two Japanese fighters chasing Lt(jg) George Ricker. Viall fired and watched the 'Zeke' dive into the water.

Les Wall's wingman, Lt(jg) Teddy L Hull, bagged two 'Zekes', one of which he literally shot out of Wall's sights. Then Wall was wounded by a 20 mm shell and forced to ditch 100 yards offshore the Russell Islands. Lt(jg) Lowell Slagle landed on the rough Russells strip, dangerously low on fuel.

The standout performance during this mission was recorded by Bill Leonard's section leader, Vern Graham, who disregarded his fuel state and remained in the combat. Although it would be Graham's only aerial encounter in his 33 missions, it would make 'Sundowner' history. In 1944 Graham told a reporter, 'I have been asked what my reactions were when I saw those Japs and realised that we were in for a life and death fight. How did I feel after waiting so long for a chance at a Nip? What were my thoughts? Frankly, I didn't have any. Or if I did I don't remember what they were. I don't think anyone going into a fight does – there are too many things to occupy one's attention. I was trying to figure out how to get into the bunch and get me a Jap before one got me. Things happen fast and decisions have to be made in split seconds'.

Graham became separated from Leonard on that first pass and from Gilbert soon thereafter. Though alone, he dived on a 'Zeke' slow-rolling behind an F4F and blew it apart with a short burst. Seconds later he met another opponent head-on.

'Then I got the surprise of my life', Graham recalled. 'He rolled over on his back and flew straight at me upside down. I had been puzzled by the first Zero's slow roll, which I hadn't yet figured out. Now this one was showing me something real nifty in aerial manoeuvring. I initially wondered if he were trying to protect himself by exposing his belly to my guns instead of his topside. But there was no time to ponder over this, or anything else, as I had to do something, and do it quickly. I fired a short burst into that exposed belly. The aeroplane never completely righted itself again. It flashed by below me and kept right on going down.'

The Sundowners' first ace made the grade the hard way – five victories in one mission. Lt(jg) Vernon E Graham was engaged in the 12 June combat near the Russells when, though low on fuel, Lt Bill Leonard led a pass at inbound Japanese raiders. In the ensuing combat Graham shot down four 'Zekes' before turning for the emergency field and finding another tailing a Corsair. Graham took a snap shot, lost sight of the enemy and made a forced landing. However, he overshot the short runway and piled into the trees. While in hospital the Marine pilot expressed his thanks and confirmed the destruction of the fifth Zero-sen (*via Tailhook Association*)

In another head-on encounter Graham saw his opponent explode in front of him, involuntarily ducking when the 'Zeke's' engine tumbled past his F4F. Graham then joined up with two Corsairs from VMF-121 and initiated an offensive weave as they attacked four 'Zekes'. One F4U drew a 'Zeke' straight across Graham's sights and his guns chopped large pieces from the Mitsubishi. After that, Graham had to give in to his rapidly diminishing fuel supply and turn his fighter toward the Russell Islands. However, yet another 'Zeke' appeared at his '12 o'clock high', so he pulled up and fired at it until the Mitsubishi fighter began to trail smoke and eventually rolled over. It was then lost to sight. At that point Graham's engine quit and two more 'Zekes' latched onto his tail. The Marines were still on hand, however, and they shot down one Zero-sen and drove the other fighter away.

Completely out of fuel, Graham made his approach to the narrow landing strip cut into the coconut plantation on Russell Island itself;

'From some recess the motor drew a little more fuel. This helped me gain speed and distance, which was fortunate, for without this added lift I wouldn't have made it. I didn't know that one of my wheels had been partly shot away and was no good for landing. When I saw I was going to make the strip, and let down the wheels and flaps, there was no indication that I was heading for trouble. As luck would have it, I struck a soft spot and the weakened wheel crumpled. My aeroplane (BuNo 12119, side number unknown) flipped over. My head struck something and I knew no more until I awakened hours later in the hospital. They told me that I had a fractured skull and a broken collarbone, but otherwise I was unhurt.

'The whole battle was hazy to me then, and I tried not to think about it. Sometime later Capt Ken Ford of VMF-121 came to see me. I didn't know him then. He said, "Nice shooting, fellow. Thanks a lot". I still didn't know what it was about. "I was in the F4U you helped out in that scrap", he said. "The one with a Jap on its tail". I nodded vaguely. "What happened to the Jap?", I enquired. "What happened to him? Why, you got him. Didn't you know?", Ford replied.'

An ace in a day, Vern Graham was awarded the Navy Cross and sent home to recover. Subsequently, he instructed in Corsairs throughout 1944 and left active duty immediately after VJ-Day.

The 'Sundowners' could now justifiably claim their self-appointed title. In the 12 June action the unit was credited with 14 'Zekes' destroyed at a cost of four F4Fs. No pilots had been lost, however. It looked like a hard record to beat, but in merely four days VF-11 would have another chance.

At 1230 hrs on 16 June, Marine fighter command alerted VF-11 to a very large Japanese formation inbound to Guadalcanal. Between 1310 hrs and 1340 hrs the 'Sundowners' scrambled seven divisions – 28 Wildcats – that dispersed to meet an estimated 120 bandits. Actually, there were 24 Aichi D3A 'Val' dive-bombers escorted by 70 'Zekes', their obvious target being American shipping crowded around the small island of Tulagi. 'Sully' Vogel, Ken Viall, Walt Hiebert and Charley Wesley's divisions went to orbit Cape Esperance, to the south of nearby Savo Island, while Frank Quady and John

Lt Raymond Vogel sits in Lt Gordon Cady's aeroplane at Guadalcanal. No 5 was the lead aircraft of the squadron's second four-aeroplane division (*via Stephen Wells*)

Ramsey's took station over the ships moored in the bay off Tulagi. Finally, Lt Cdr White and his flight of four F4Fs started patrolling directly overhead Guadalcanal's Henderson Field.

By swinging wide to the southwest, the Japanese eluded early interception from the Russells and were reported only 25 miles south of 'Fighter One' at 1400 hrs, heading northeast. Frank Quady was the first to sight the dive-bombers, with 'Zekes' deployed on either flank at 15,000 ft, and he led Lt(jg)s Henry 'Sol' White, Charles H 'Red' Schild and John A Cooke out of the sun in high overhead and stern runs. Quady recounted the action;

'We were at 25,000 ft and the enemy consisted of two shallow vees of nine or ten dive-bombers each, with a column of Zeros slightly above and on either side. There were 25 to 30 Zeros, and I made a stern run into the leading vee of bombers, shooting at the second aeroplane from the right end. The dive-bomber began to smoke and fell off to the right. Meanwhile, the end aeroplane pulled up to avoid the damaged "Val" and I gave him a burst. He immediately shuddered, smoked and followed his companion down.

'I then pulled up and around and went into a head-on with a Zero. I emptied the rest of my ammunition into him and he smoked and fell downward. I received three 20 mm cannon shots and numerous 7.7s and spun down too. With a Zero following, I went into a cloud, where I stayed until the field was clear. There was a Mitsubishi twin-engined bomber also flying around in the cloud, and I tried to give him a burst but my ammunition was exhausted. My controls were all but shot away and I thought of bailing out, but finally made the field.'

Lt(jg) White related his part of the engagement;

'I peeled off after Lt Quady and opened up on the "Val" on the inside of the formation. My burst hit him in the right wing, which sheared off. He went straight into the mountain on the right. I then put about 100 rounds into the third aeroplane from the end, breaking off when he began to emit heavy smoke and fall off to the right.'

Lt(jg) John Ramsey, approaching the Japanese from the northwest with a considerable altitude advantage, exploited it fully;

'I had taken a division that included one pilot on the sick list, another who had been on the ground for three weeks awaiting transfer and a third who had been shot down nine days previously and had been back with the squadron for less than a week.

'All I could see around me were Zeros and three F4Fs. Several Zeros made passes at me and one made a beautiful overhead run. I gave him a burst and he erupted in flames and fell away.

'I looked around to find a cream-coloured dive-bomber with black markings burning merrily, with a Wildcat on his tail – the "Val" was almost flying in formation with me. I saw two more of the same type, and although my motor was smoking and oil was being splattered over the windshield, I managed to give the second one a burst and he burned. I was wondering whether to bail out, but the Zeros around and the AA bursts dissuaded me from jumping, and I came in making a dead-stick landing.'

Lt(jg) John Pressler claimed two 'Zekes' but then landed BuNo 11937 in the water with sudden engine stoppage.

Lt Cdr White contacted the dive-bombers just as they pushed over on the ships 15,000 ft below. White and his wingman, Teddy Hull, went after the 'Vals' in line astern, and the CO hit two that fell away smoking, which he claimed as probables. After a brief tussle with a 'Zeke', White looked around and Hull was nowhere in sight.

White's second section had a field day, with Lt(jg)s Charlie Stimpson and Jim Swope making repeated runs on the diving 'Vals'. Both men did nearly as well as Vern Graham had four days before, with 'Skull' Stimpson splashing four dive-bombers and Swope three. They were the first kills for either pilot, both of whom would ultimately become aces.

Despite his inexperience in aerial combat, Swope found room for reflection in a postwar account of the action;

This photograph was taken late in the squadron's Guadalcanal tour, and the 48 victory flags on the propeller blades suggests mid-June 1943. The middle blade also shows six purple hearts in testament to the 'Sundowners'' casualties. The 33 pilots seen here are short of the full roster, since four Naval Aviators (Dayhoff, Graber, Graham and Slagle) had been evacuated due to wounds or illness. In the front row, from left to right, are Cary, Gilbert, Schild, Wesley, Ramsey, H S White, Coppola and Jones. In the front row, standing, from left to right, are Hiebert, Leonard, Wall, Cady (behind left prop), Pimentel, Johnson and Viall. In the rear two rows, from left to right, are Parker, Holberton, Ogilvie, Flath, Ivie, Gaston, Work, Martin, Cooke, Stimpson, Swope, Masoner, Hubler and Hubbard (*via Tailhook Association*)

'While working on some Aichi dive-bombers I had the misfortune to become engaged singly with a Zero. I couldn't get a single lick in at the "Zeke", but my F4F took two explosive 20 mm cannon shells and close to 40 7.7 mm bullets. Three cylinders were blown off the engine, but I evaded the Jap and still flew that battered F4F 20 miles back to "Fighter One", and the scrap heap.'

Despite the best efforts of VF-11, two US ships had been hit by bombs, after which the 'Vals' fled north at low level. Vogel's 16 Wildcats slammed into the combat over the Savo-Tulagi-Lunga area and the sky was immediately filled with dogfights from 20,000 ft on down. Lt Kenneth T Viall knocked two 'Vals' into the water, then got a 'Zeke'. Lt(jg) William J Masoner claimed two 'Zekes', and he subsequently added ten more kills to his tally with VF-19 in 1944. VF-11 suffered losses too, however, as Lt(jg)s George Ricker and Chandler Boswell collided and crashed into the sea as they pursued a 'Zeke' low over the water. Both pilots were lost in BuNos 11899 and 4095, respectively.

Then it was over. American fighters wheeled around, temporarily alerted by a false alarm of more bogies, before landing at Henderson Field and the two fighter strips. It was thought that 94 of the estimated 120 enemy aircraft had been downed, with VF-11 claiming 31 – the largest share of the kills. Since it is known that the Japanese despatched exactly 94 aeroplanes, there was obviously an element of overclaiming, but not very much. The Japanese formation was almost annihilated, losing the equivalent of almost two carrier air groups in terms of the number of aircraft shot down.

In return for 31 kills by 17 of the 28 'Sundowners' participating in the mission, four Wildcats and three pilots were gone. The losses were another indication of VF-11's major role in the battle, as only two other US fighters were destroyed. Lt(jg) John G Pressler made it safely to shore from his ditched F4F, and USAAF pilots reported a P-40 colliding with a Wildcat – almost certainly Teddy Hull in BuNo 11899. Apparently none of the three missing 'Sundowners' fell to enemy aircraft. Collision was the often unavoidable result of so many aeroplanes being crowded into a limited airspace.

Rear Adm Marc Mitscher, Commander Air Forces Solomons (ComAirSols), was so appreciative of VF-11's contribution to the record victory that he sent two cases of whiskey to the unit by way of congratulation. The 'Sundowners' employed Mitscher's gift to convince two war correspondents that 'Fighting 11' was the only outfit on Guadalcanal worth writing about. A convoluted press account later identified the 'Sundowners' as 'squadron 11', and attributed all 94 victories claimed on that date to VF-11! Despite that lapse, one memorable line was penned when Stimpson was dubbed 'Trigger Mortis'.

A single kill was registered on 21 June when Lt(jg) Homer Schild of Frank Quady's division found a G3M 'Nell' bomber near Santa Isabel. Separated from the others, Schild made three passes and shot the aircraft down for his third victory. But VF-11 lost another fighter when Lt(jg) Henry White, the colourful West Virginian, overshot the runway while making a forced landing and nosed into the Tenaru River. Long flying hours, heavy combat and general fatigue were taking their toll. Despite the fact that VF-11's excellent mechanics had presented the unit with a 'new' Wildcat built from spares, both aircraft and pilot availability declined. Dan Hubbard wiped out an F4F in a landing accident around this time too, damaging three others, and he was evacuated with injuries.

JULY ACTIONS

Adm Mitscher said that VF-11 was due for rotation at this time, but not immediately. On 6 July the 'Sundowners' escorted TBFs to Kula Gulf and a division composed of Lt Charles V Wesley, Lt(jgs) Chester A Parker, Charlie Stimpson and Jim Swope tangled with six to eight 'Zekes'. The Japanese pilots must have held a grudge against Texans, as they all tied on to Swope's tail. Stimpson destroyed one from directly astern, while Wesley and Parker made overhead runs on the others as Swope engaged in violent aerobatics. A superior airman, Swope shook the 'Zekes' after Wesley and Parker had each downed one. Swope than bagged a 'Zeke' himself, but his Wildcat was so badly shot up that it was declared fit only for scrapping upon his return to base.

'Fighting 11's' last combat at Guadalcanal occurred three days later on 9 July when Lt Cdrs White and Vogel led two divisions on a combat air patrol (CAP) over Rendova. An estimated 40+ 'Zekes' in two waves were reported, but Bob Flath developed a rough engine so Bill Masoner was ordered to escort him home. In the dogfight 'Skull' Stimpson repeated his performance of three days earlier by shooting a 'Zeke' off Jim Swope's tail, who shared in the destruction of two bandits with Clarence White and Vern Gaston.

But the engagement was not all one-sided, as White glimpsed an F4F in a vertical dive off Rendova. It was Cy Cary, Vogel's wingman, who failed to return in BuNo 11944. Vogel was also hit, taking three 20 mm shells in one wing.

The 'Sundowners' continued the strenuous Rendova CAPs until dusk on 11 July. The missions averaged three-and-a-half hours in duration, and some pilots occasionally flew two such sorties in a single

Raymond 'Sully' Vogel in the cockpit of his assigned F4F-4, which carried the side number F17. As executive officer he led the second half of the squadron, although at one time the 'Sundowners' had nearly 40 aircraft, including spares (*via Stephen Wells*)

day, logging up to eight hours in the air – much of it on oxygen. Finally, on the 12th, VF-11 launched from 'Fighter One' for the last time when it commenced its deployment south from 'Cactus', homeward bound.

In 11 weeks the squadron had been credited with 55 enemy aircraft destroyed – 37 'Zekes', 17 'Vals' and a solitary 'Nell'. Five pilots had been killed, but only Cary was lost to enemy aircraft. Three others (Maxwell, Graham and Hubbard) were evacuated with injuries. Twelve Wildcats had been lost in aerial combat for a kill-loss ratio of 4.5-to-1. Probably another six F4Fs had been destroyed in accidents, and two more were written off after suffering extensive battle damage.

In their first tour the 'Sundowners' had produced two aces – Stimpson with six kills and Graham with five. Swope came perilously close with 4.66. Additionally, Bill Leonard added his fifth and sixth victories of the war. Graham may have identified the source of VF-11's success when he said, 'Many times I was grateful for the opportunity of flying with so many well-trained, talented Regular Navy men'. Fenton, White, Cady and the others had done their jobs well – the results proved it.

ComAirSols agreed, for on 18 July Rear Adm Marc Mitscher issued the following commendation to CAG-11;

'The operations of the past three months have been noteworthy for the aggressive manner in which offensive and defensive missions have been executed.

'I desire to convey to the pilots and to all personnel, air and ground alike, my most heartfelt "well done" for the outstanding performance of duty which has characterised the entire period of its service under my command at Guadalcanal.

'To the living, I say no unit has excelled you in exacting from the enemy the maximum toll for your honoured dead.'

Furthermore, the six non-flying officers were recommended for the Legion of Merit, while the 82 chief petty officers and enlisted men also earned commendations.

During a two-week stop at Espiritu Santo the pilots encountered the aeroplane most of them yearned for, the F6F-3 Hellcat. Bill Leonard and some others were anxious to try out the new Grumman fighters, which were being accumulated for VF-12. 'The F6F-3 was almost as good as the F4U in fighter performance, and was alleged to be as good as the F4F in carrier behaviour', Leonard recalled. After flying the Hellcats, he and some of the other VF-11 pilots hoped to be taking them to Guadalcanal to give the type its combat debut, but it was not to be.

The squadron boarded *Chenango* in early August and arrived at NAS Alameda on the 21st. Many of the pilots were dispersed and assigned to other duties. Quady and Leonard, who had completed their second tours, went to Mitscher's staff at ComAirWestCoast, Cdr White joined the staff of ComAirPac and Vogel returned to Annapolis for medical treatment and subsequent duty at the Naval Academy. Both finished the war as air group commanders. Gordon Cady was promoted to lieutenant commander and took over as CO of VF-11, effective 25 September 1943.

Lt Bill Leonard receives a belated Air Medal from Adm Marc Mitscher in late 1943. VF-11 had served under Mitscher when he was ComAirSols earlier that year (*via Rich Leonard*)

WITH THE FAST CARRIERS

In the summer of 1943 the 'Sundowners' began a training and reforming cycle with a nucleus of veterans such as Stimpson, Swope, Henry White, John Ramsey and a few others. At the same time some SBD Dauntless pilots who had flown with Bombing and Scouting 11 (redesignated VB-21) at Guadalcanal transferred into Cady's unit. One such Naval Aviator was Lt(jg) Robert Saggau, an All-American halfback from the 1938-40 Notre Dame football team. Saggau and the other dive-bomber pilots simply decided they wanted a chance to fly fighters, and the swap 'was actually very simple', he recalled. 'We requested through channels to transfer to VF-11 and were so authorised'.

A pilot who had a harder time getting transferred in was the new executive officer, Lt Eugene G Fairfax. A determined, aggressive

Lt Eugene G Fairfax joined VF-11 in September 1943 during 'turnaround' training in California. Previously a floatplane pilot, he managed a transfer to fighters and became executive officer to Cdr Gordon Cady. A year later Cady was transferred to TF-38 staff and Fairfax 'fleeted up' to skipper. As a lieutenant commander he retained command until after the *Hornet* deployment in 1945, and subsequently returned to lead the squadron in 1946. Fairfax eventually retired as a rear admiral (*via Tailhook Association*)

27-year-old, Fairfax had enlisted in the US Navy in 1934 and entered Annapolis in 1935. Eventually becoming captain of the boxing team, he graduated in 1939, ranking 176th of 581 cadets. First assigned to battleships, Fairfax transferred to aviation and received his wings in March 1942. He flew OS2U Kingfisher floatplanes from USS *Tennessee* (BB-43), but soon tired of the relatively tame life of an observation pilot and, in the words of the fleet air personnel officer, 'stuck out his neck about 40 ft' by going out of channels to request a transfer to fighters.

The request was granted and Gene Fairfax joined VF-11 in September 1943. Although he arrived with 675 hours in his logbook, his work was cut out for him. The phrase 'arrogant fighter pilots' has been overworked, but some 'Sundowners'' initial reaction to receiving an OS2U pilot as 'exec' was less than enthusiastic. However, Gordon Cady was on top of the situation, as he had Jim Swope introduce Fairfax to the fighter pilots. Before long the new XO was accepted by the old hands.

Some of the middle-grade pilots came from instructing duty, such as Lt(jg) Jimmie E Savage, the easy-going Texan who had studied economics in college. He pinned on his wings in November 1941 and, after service as a 'plowback' instructor, joined VF-11 in October 1943. He was promptly designated engineering officer.

Cady gave Jim Swope his pick of the new ensigns for a wingman, and Swope selected Horace B Moranville, a 20-year-old Nebraskan who had quit college when the flying bug bit. But the new pilots were not all reservists. Lt(jg) Robert E Clements, the flight officer, had been a year behind Fairfax at Annapolis, graduating in the upper quarter of his class and subsequently serving aboard the battleship USS *Pennsylvania* (BB-38) at Pearl Harbor. He was just six months out of Pensacola when he joined VF-11. Originally assigned to SBDs, Clements had gone to Bill Leonard in San Diego to arrange a transfer to VF-11.

The squadron trained on F4F-4s until early October, when F6F-3s became available. Not long after acquiring Hellcats, the 'Sundowners' also acquired a mascot. All pilots had to qualify on the pistol range, and the small-arms instructor gave Gordon Cady one of a litter of Boston

Enjoying a night out, these VF-11 pilots have donned their dress blue uniforms for the occasion. They are sitting, from left to right, Bud Brown, Mary Lou and Terry Holberton, Mary and Charlie Stimpson, Pearl and Bob Flath and Mary and Tom Adams (the latter from VT-11). Standing, from left to right, are Gordon Cady, 'Smiley' Johnson, Betty Brown, Mrs Cady and Dave (from VB-11) and Yvonne Braden. Lt(jg) James S 'Bud' Brown had previously flown SBDs in VB-21 and, like several dive-bomber pilots, asked to transition to fighters (*via Tailhook Association*)

This Hellcat seems to be a VF-11 aircraft flying in the Hawaiian Islands during the squadron's 'work-up' period in 1944. The Sundowners emblem was seldom applied to F6Fs until the end of the *Hornet* cruise (*via Steve Wells*)

Bull Terrier pups. The dog was christened 'Gunner' and Cady delegated Blake Moranville, then the youngest pilot in the squadron, to be its caretaker. Blake and 'Gunner' soon became inseparable.

In January 1944 VF-11 moved briefly to Crow's Landing, California, for night flying, then back to Alameda in February for initial carrier qualifications aboard the escort carrier USS *Copahee* (CVE-12), at which point 'Gunner' first tried his sea legs. Finally, in late March, following a seven-month 'turnaround', the reorganised CAG-11 deployed to Hawaii with aircraft aboard the new fleet carrier USS *Wasp* (CV-18). When 'Fighting 11' went ashore once again, Cady initiated an intensive training programme. In order to obtain maximum experience from each flight, three divisions took off before dawn on most days for an average of three hours. Thus, the schedule provided night flying and navigation. One division acted as bombers while the other two practiced escort techniques based on Cady's 'roving weave'. The 12 Hellcats also conducted air-to-air and air-to-ground gunnery at the firing range before turning for home.

An added touch of realism was provided whenever a radar director could vector the 'Sundowners' onto a formation of USAAF fighters, most often Seventh Air Force P-47s. The Hellcats usually had the best of the mock combats, for an F6F could nearly always turn inside a Thunderbolt, although the 'Jugs' were noticeably faster. Other practice missions included 'group gropes' with VB-11's SB2C Helldivers and VT-11's TBM Avengers.

Subsequent moves were made to Maui and Hilo, with more carrier landings in July aboard USS *Kadashan Bay* (CVE-76). The air group spent a total of five months working up in Hawaii, which to some eager youngsters such as Blake 'Rabbit' Moranville seemed 'like forever'. But the time was made immensely more pleasant as the 'Sundowners' renewed their friendship with the von Tempskys. The first-tour pilots were well acquainted with the family, and the 'nuggets' soon felt at home on the sprawling estate. So much so that three 'Sundowners' were constantly at the plantation, rotating every two days when the relief arrived in three F6Fs.

Cady and the crew presented Alexa with a four-star flag symbolic of her position as 'ComWolfPack', and whenever the ensign was flown it was interpreted as the all-clear signal for arriving pilots to indulge in a spectacular buzz job. If the flag was not visible, it meant that potentially unappreciative visitors were aboard, and the pilots were to conduct themselves as Congress intended for officers and gentlemen.

In mid-August Gordon Cady was relieved as CO and ordered to Rear Adm John McCain's staff with Task Force (TF) 38. Gene Fairfax, now a lieutenant commander, took over and Bob Clements became

Cdr Gordon Cady (front centre) is seen at a squadron party, probably at Barbers Point, Hawaii, in mid August 1944. Other pilots in this photograph are, from left to right, Dick Cyr, unknown, Jake Robcke (in cap), Bud Brown, Danny Work, possibly 'Doc' Savage and future CO Gene Fairfax. Cady was killed in an F6F accident while on the fast carrier staff later that month (*via Tim Enander*)

executive officer. They only had about three weeks to settle into their new jobs before shipping out, as the air group had orders for the Western Pacific. A final few deck landings were made aboard USS *Ranger* (CV-4) in the first few days of September.

The squadron was divided for the trip west, with the maintenance personnel, minus aircraft, boarding *Wasp*, while most officers were delegated the entirely unwelcome chore of serving as armed guards on a transport ship loaded with former convicts from the US Navy prison at Treasure Island. CAG-11, under Cdr Frederick R Schrader, was reunited at Manus Harbour, in the Admiralties, during mid-September. Gene Fairfax had 45 pilots – young men from 33 of the 48 states ranging in age from 19 to 28.

CAG Schrader held impressive credentials, having graduated 35th of 442 in the Annapolis class of 1935. He commanded VF-3, but was detached in late August to take over CAG-11.

During the turnaround and work-up cycle the 'Sundowners' had lost seven Hellcats and one pilot, Ens T B Reed in Hawaii. But the attrition was less than many squadrons sustained, and there was seldom a shortage of operational aircraft as Grumman delivered hundreds of new

Pilots in flight gear before the *Hornet* cruise. Those marked with an asterisk denote that they were killed during the deployment. In the front row, from left to right, are Zink, Dayhoff*, Hardy, Savage, Lloyd, Meyers, Zoecklein, Fairfax, Cady, Lee*, Clements, Willis, Crusoe, Sims, Ramsey and McBride. In the middle row, from left to right, are Parsons, Saggau, Warren, Flath, Blair*, Stimpson, Suddreth, Swope, Cyr, Williams, White, Groves, Goldberg*, Chase*, Morris and Robcke. And in the rear row, from left to right, are Lizotte, Boring*, Richardson, Dance*, Ptacket*, Hintze, Derolf*, Moranville, Coeur, C D Smith, Parsley, Bratcres*, Holberton, James and Farley (*Tim Enander*)

Aircraft carrier crews seldom miss a chance for a ceremonial cake, and each thousandth arrested landing offers a suitable occasion. Here squadron CO Lt Cdr Gene Fairfax presents Lt Bud Brown with a cake for making *Hornet's* 10,000th landing on 12 October 1944 (*via Tailhook Association*)

The 'Sundowners'' second combat deployment was carrier-based in USS *Hornet* (CV-12) from October 1944 through January 1945 (*via Tailhook Association*)

Hellcats each month. From October 1943 through to August 1944, most VF-11 pilots averaged 40 hours per month. Stimpson, for instance, accumulated 422 hours in that time, returning to combat with 415 hours 'in type'. The more senior pilots had logged between 900 and 1200 hours total time.

Seven 'Sundowners' remained from the Guadalcanal tour – Nelson Dayhoff, Bob 'Cac' Flath, John Ramsey, Charlie Stimpson, Jim Swope, Henry White and Dan Work. Schrader's squadrons were to replace CAG-2 aboard USS *Hornet* (CV-12), and they received most of their initial aircraft from the veteran units within that air group. 'Fighting 11' inherited VF-2's Hellcats, which were a mixture of F6F-3s and -5s, all sporting *Hornet's* white ball marking on the tail. A nightfighter detachment flying radar-equipped Hellcats was permanently assigned to the vessel as well, and it would share some of VF-11's facilities aboard ship.

At Manus *Hornet's* skipper, Capt A K 'Artie' Doyle, welcomed the new fliers aboard, and he used the time available to exercise the air group at sea. Gordon Cady, meanwhile, had been conscientiously working on an operations plan for the Fast Carrier Task Force and, though fatigued from long hours, he flew from carrier to carrier putting his customary personal touch on the preparations. On 30 August, when landing aboard USS *Belleau Wood* (CVL-24), his arresting hook broke and his aeroplane slammed inverted into the barrier. Cady died in the crash. His loss was a serious blow to the 'Sundowners', as he had led the squadron for almost a year. Cady was replaced as task force assistant operations officer by his friend Bill Leonard.

Shortly after the air group reported aboard, *Hornet's* landing signal officers (LSOs) explained their preferences to all pilots. Standard operating procedure was to defer landings until all combat air patrol or antisubmarine flights had returned to the ship. The advice stressed 'Do not try to follow the deck when in the groove but try to maintain a steady approach. Do not take your own wave-off because you think you are too close to the preceding aeroplane. In general, most pilots should make their approach in the groove a little longer in spacing.

The LSO should be able to pick you up and start working you immediately after cutting or waving off the aeroplane ahead of you'.

In the event of battle damage, low fuel or engine trouble, early arrivals were permitted to enter the pattern before rendezvous was complete, provided they received a 'Charlie' signal light (Morse Code letter C, 'dash-dot-dash-dot').

Hornet's senior LSO was Lt Doug Carter, who earned tremendous respect from VF-11. Ens Jack 'Soapy' Suddreth, said, 'I know I would not have been able to get aboard with my damaged aeroplane without his help. Thanks to Doug Carter I survived'.

As with any new air group, it took some time for the squadrons to adjust to the carrier's way of operating, but Schrader's pilots began reducing their landing intervals – the mark of tailhook professionalism.

TF-38 sortied from Manus in early October, taking CAG-11 to war 15 months after leaving Guadalcanal. But it was over a week to the operating area, and there were other distractions. On the 4th former Guadalcanal SBD pilot Lt James S 'Bud' Brown made *Hornet's* 10,000th landing, and Capt Doyle presented the 'Sundowners' with a cake to mark the occasion. The next day Ens S J Richardson was forced to ditch BuNo 58417 with a broken oil line. He suffered a slight cut on the head but was rescued by a destroyer.

On 9 October 1944 Gene Fairfax counted 46 Hellcats available, including at least 15 new F6F-5s. He was going to need them, because the next day would be VF-11's first combat mission from *Hornet*. The target was Japanese shipping in the Nansei Shoto group between Okinawa and Japan.

The fourth fighter mission of 10 October demonstrated VF-11's proficiency, even though nearly all the unit's pilots were new to combat. The 'Sundowners' averaged 19 seconds between each launch, which was only a quarter of a second off *Hornet's* record. This performance prompted the carrier's air department to send a 'Really hot' teletype to each ready room.

Armed with bombs and rockets, the F6Fs went in low over Miyako Jima's anchorage to get at enemy shipping. Lt J E 'Doc' Savage took his division down on a 5500-ton transport, pressing through AA fire to

The 'Sundowners' before deploying in *Hornet* in October 1944. Enlisted sailors sat in the front row, from left to right, are Rouse, Eaton, Saville, Hamptom, Donaldson, Cluck, Theimer, Berry, Manthey, Watson, Reich, Butterly, Edwards, Bell, Clayton and Brouillard. Officers in the second row, from left to right, are Hardy, Dayhoff*, Flath, Holberton, Ramsey, Savage, Crusoe, Fairfax, Cady, Clements, Meyers, Griffin, Lee*, Swope, Martin and Parsley. Officers in the third row, from left to right, are Lloyd, Bratcres*, Goldberg*, MacBride, Morris, White, Cyr, Stimpson, Saggau, Dance*, Coeur, Hintze, Zink, James, Moranville and Boring*. And officers in the rear row, from left to right, are Smith, Warren, Willis, Chase*, Robcke, Groves, Sims, Ptacket*, Nellis, Meade, Suddreth, Farley, Williams, Blair*, Parsons, Lizotte, Zoeckleim and Derolf*. Again, those names marked with an asterisk indicate pilots killed during the deployment (*via Tim Enander*)

Enlisted men of the air group's three squadrons photographed off Hawaii sometime between March and September 1944. Each squadron possessed sailors skilled in a variety of specialties – engine mechanics, metal smiths, ordnancemen and radio-electronics experts. Additionally, each aircraft carrier had an organic maintenance department to perform work beyond the capabilities of the air group (*via Tailhook Association*)

skip-bomb the vessel. Ens Ken Chase, the baby of the squadron, got a direct hit with his 500-lb bomb, but was almost immediately shot off Savage's wing in BuNo 70130. Finally, Lt John Ramsey and Lt(jg) W H Boring rocketed a destroyer tender that beached itself and burned. VF-11 had probably sunk two ships, although Ken Chase was lost. Said Jack Suddreth, 'Quite a blow to us all'.

Ens George Lindesmith evened the score when he caught a 'Val' dive-bomber and shot it down – the first aerial kill of the cruise.

Operations continued the next day, and VF-11 proved the near-record launch on the 10th was no fluke. Thirty-one Hellcats and three SB2Cs were launched with an average 17.5 seconds separation. The teletype in the ready room clacked out a message, 'The boys set a new record on that launch. The captain is tickled'.

On 12 October the Fast Carrier Task Force went to work farther south, sending strikes against Formosa. The day's first fighter mission launched at 0545 hrs for Takao and Hieto. The 'Sundowners' damaged some shipping, but were mostly concerned with shooting up airfields. Ens Lindesmith, who had notched the first aerial victory of the cruise only two days before, was last seen strafing Hieto Airfield in BuNo 58234. VF-11 executive officer Lt Cdr Bob Clements recorded the second kill by downing a Ki-43 'Oscar'. Lt(jg) G L Morris was the only other pilot to engage, claiming a Ki-61 'Tony' probably destroyed.

The next day was Friday the 13th, and it proved to be no joke. Things started badly when a nightfighter Hellcat landed with its guns charged, and the bump on recovering aboard the ship set off several rounds. Another night Hellcat and some SB2Cs were damaged.

Strike 1C launched shortly before 1300 hrs against Takao City, led by the CAG, Cdr Schrader. 'Doc' Savage described the attack;

'My division and Lt Nelson W Dayhoff's took off from *Hornet* 30 minutes before dawn and formed up with two other divisions of fighters from *Wasp*. We proceeded toward Formosa, some 175 miles away, setting our course for Hieto airfield at 12,500 ft. Our primary mission was to shoot down airborne aircraft – secondary was to destroy aeroplanes on the ground.

'Things were uneventful until we crossed the range of mountains on the extreme eastern side of the island. Hieto lay just the other side of those mountains, and we had hardly passed over the top when the AA started. We flew around awhile, weaving back and forth by divisions, looking for airborne opposition. None could be found, so I took my divisions down to strafe.

'Hieto was one of the major airfields on Formosa, serving as a staging field for the Philippines, so ground targets were plentiful there. The AA was heavy so we dove by divisions at a 55-degree angle using full throttle from 12,000 ft, levelling off by 1000 ft. I noticed two Jap aeroplanes milling around above us, dropping phosphorous bombs at our formation just before each strafing run. On our sixth pass they came down after my division – one of them (a Ki-44 "Tojo") made a run on me but overshot as I cut my throttle completely. He had so much speed from diving that he couldn't stay behind me. As he shot by I added full throttle and dove with him as he split-essed to the deck. He levelled off at 500 ft and I closed to 800 ft and fired my six 0.50-cals from dead astern. He started a roll, but flamed while on his back, dove straight for the ground burning and exploded on hitting the deck.

'I formed my division up quickly and sent one section home, as the leader had been hit by AA on the last strafing run. I took some pictures of the nine burning aeroplanes on the field, as I had a photo-F6F that morning.

'I left Hieto then and proceeded north to Okoyama airfield, which is also used for staging aircraft, as well as being home to the largest and most important aeroplane assembly plant on Formosa. B-29s from China had made one night raid on the field, so the Japs had AA guns everywhere around this area. I had Lt Dayhoff's division cover me while I took photographs with my oblique camera at 1500 ft. They stayed at 8000 ft, drawing part of the AA fire. After getting the required pictures, we started strafing ground targets and fired seven transport aeroplanes before my wingman was hit by AA.

'We immediately formed up the three remaining divisions and headed for home. I wanted to get my pictures back, as the B-29s from China were scheduled for another night raid and would need the information. We landed aboard *Hornet* at 0930 hrs.'

The otherwise successful strike was marred by the loss of Cdr Schrader, whose Hellcat (BuNo 58192) crashed while strafing Toko seaplane base. His wingman, Ens J P Sims, reported that the CAG's aeroplane was struck by light AA fire.

Late that same evening Ens Leon Lee ditched BuNo 70400 when he ran out of fuel in *Hornet's* landing pattern. He could not be located in the dark, and a daylight search was fruitless too.

14 October proved to be one of the 'Sundowners'' best days, and one of its worst. The first loss occurred at 0430 hrs when Lt Edward Helgerson's F6F-5N (BuNo 58167) taxied off the flightdeck in the

CAG-11 sailed to Hawaii in March 1944, remaining for six months of precombat training. While there VF-11 perfected squadron tactics and flew numerous 'group gropes', integrating operations with VB-11's SB2C Helldivers and VT-11's TBM Avengers. These Naval Aviators flew the aircraft assigned to all three units (*via Tailhook Association*)

dark. The early sweep found airborne targets, resulting in claims for a 'Tony' destroyed and a second fighter as a probable, but Ens Henry Ptacket (BuNo 58828) was last seen engaged with another Ki-61. Later that morning the CAP splashed two D4Y 'Judy' dive-bombers and a P1Y1 'Frances' bomber.

The day's main encounter occurred when seven Hellcats, led by 'Nellie' Dayhoff and 'Doc' Savage, were vectored onto a large enemy formation approaching Task Group 38.1 at 1420 hrs. Savage described the action that followed;

'Enemy aeroplanes had kept us up at general quarters all night. None of us slept. Next morning found my and Dayhoff's divisions in the ready room in "Condition 11" (airborne in ten minutes). Around noon we were scrambled and sent to 10,000 ft by the fighter director. I immediately received a vector of "275 degrees, bogey '12 o'clock', 80 miles". After several minutes the director said, "Vector port 265 degrees, bogey 'one o'clock', angels 18, 50 miles". After flying about 50 miles from the task force, I tally-hoed many bogies "two o'clock up" at 15 miles. The Fighter Direction Officer said, "Attack, and good luck".

'I counted 34 aeroplanes and called back for help, climbing for altitude. We made our initial attack out of the sun with about a 1000-ft advantage. Lt Charles Stimpson was leading Lt Dayhoff's division as Dayhoff's radio wasn't working. He went after the dive-bombers with his division and I took the fighters just astern of the bombers. Stimpson flamed three bombers (actually "Hamps" – author) before they knew we were there. I closed on two "Zekes" and flamed them.

'As I moved to the left on another section I saw tracers come by my wing. I turned very steeply but the Jap had the advantage and I couldn't out-turn him. He couldn't hit me, however, because he couldn't get enough lead. After several turns, Lt Stimpson saw him and came over and shot the Jap down. I dove on two more Jap fighters but missed and overshot. I came back but they had gone, so I climbed for more altitude. I looked down and noticed several aeroplanes going down in flames.

'I turned left and saw two more aeroplanes closing on me from astern. They split and I was boxed with one on either side. I turned right, but the one on the left immediately started hitting me. One 12.7 mm round shattered the instrument panel and I split-essed, rolling to the right and going straight down at full throttle. I dove from 15,000 ft to 500 ft and pulled out, noticing streamers coming off my wings, but the Japs were still after me. I headed for some clouds 15 miles away, and at approximately 5000 ft I managed to gain distance on the Japs by using full power. I was also forced to gain altitude at a very slow rate, otherwise I'd have lost too much speed in climbing.

'I reached the clouds and got in them okay, but I wasn't in the cloud bank very long before I was in real trouble as my instruments weren't working. The needle and ball was shot away and I had tumbled my gyro-horizon when I split-essed and rolled on the way down. After awhile I got into a spin but recovered by sheer luck as I kicked the rudder against the way I thought I was spinning, and sure enough that was right.'

After the initial attack in which Stimpson downed three Zero-sens and his wingman, Ens Fred Blair, another, both formations had been

Lt Jimmie E Savage was a former instructor who joined VF-11 in September 1943. As a division leader he often flew photo-reconnaissance missions, but still found the opportunity to engage enemy aircraft. Indeed, Savage was credited with seven victories between October and December 1944 (*via Henk van der Lugt*)

Lt Charlie Stimpson finished the war as the 'Sundowners'' ranking ace with 16 victories. He was one of a handful of Naval Aviators who scored five or more kills in both the F4F and F6F. 'Skull' Stimpson became one of the deadliest fighter pilots in naval service, usually scoring in multiples, including five and four victories in a day. He remains the US Navy's seventh ranking fighter ace of all time, tied with Lt Ira Kepford of VF-17 and Lt(jg) Douglas Baker of VF-20 (*via Tailhook Association*)

Lt Charlie Stimpson and his wingman, Ens Fred Blair, who was lost in the 14 October 1944 combat off Formosa. In that lopsided dogfight Stimpson claimed five kills and Blair was credited with three, but the latter then had to ditch his damaged Hellcat and he went down with the aircraft (*via Steve Wells*)

broken up. Stimpson and Blair then scissored on each other and 'Skull' got bursts into two 'Tonys' that smoked and fell away. Blair returned the favour by flaming a 'Zeke' behind his leader, then gunned two more. Reversing his turn, Stimpson saw yet another 'Zeke' firing at Blair, hitting him badly. Stimpson fired at wide deflection and blew a wing off the 'Zeke' for his fifth kill of the combat.

'Blair had been hit and I saw his belly tank was on fire', Stimpson later recalled. 'I told him to drop it and dive for the deck. I crossed over him but only one "Zeke" attempted to follow, and he was scared off when I fired my remaining ammunition in front of him'. Stimpson then watched his wingman ditch the crippled Hellcat, which sank quickly in the rough sea. Fred Blair did not get out of BuNo 43137.

Back aboard *Hornet* noses were counted and the hassle was evaluated. Three other pilots were missing. Lt(jg) Sam Goldberg in BuNo 70454 was never seen again after the fight began and his wingman, Ens Ted Lepianka, wounded in one shoulder, flopped BuNo 58950 onto the deck without flaps or wheels. 'Nellie' Dayhoff, one of the Guadalcanal veterans, was also missing. His number two, Lt(jg) John A Zink, reported that both had splashed 'Judys' on the first pass, but were then jumped from above. Dayhoff destroyed one 'Zeke' and Zink torched another 'Judy' before the former was hit from above by a second Zero-sen. Zink followed his leader down to the water, watching him crash in BuNo 70544.

'Doc' Savage returned well after the others. Without an operable compass, and after outrunning his pursuers for some 25 miles, he made an educated guess of the reciprocal course by judging the sun angle. After one hour and 45 minutes he found a destroyer that directed some CAP fighters to escort him home. With emotion in his voice Savage related, 'I landed aboard, having been given up for lost after being two hours overdue. The fellows gave me a royal welcome. I was so happy to get home I just couldn't hold back the tears. I think all hands understood how I felt'.

The final verdict on the combat was 14 definite kills and two probables for the loss of three pilots and four aircraft. The day's full tally was 18 victories against five 'Sundowners' and six Hellcats.

Events of the 14th sparked understandably mixed emotions. Stimpson exulted in his logbook, 'Five flamers! Probably destroyed two'. But much later he reflected that the squadron's losses were only acceptable because they were incurred in preventing a major attack on the task force.

Like Charlie Stimpson, Ens William G Eccles hailed from Utah. While flying CAP on 14 October he scored his first victory (a 'Judy') in the same action that Stimpson made 'ace in a day'. Subsequently, Eccles was among the replacements sent to VF-18 for about four weeks. *Intrepid's* (CV-11) Hellcats had taken some heavy losses, losing four or more pilots in a day. While detached, Eccles claimed three victories, then returned to *Hornet* to complete his deployment – some sources list him as an ace, but his career total was four kills.

The 15th yielded four victories as the enemy tried to penetrate the task group's aerial pickets. The day began with a 'Frances' splashed by the CAP, but more losses ensued. In the afternoon Ens O L Jacobsen wiped out BuNo 58044 when he hit *Hornet's* island in a landing accident – the pilot escaped injury. However, that evening a CAP action west of the task force cost VF-11 Ens Robert C Dance. He splashed one of three 'Judys' claimed in the interception, but in turn was shot down and bailed out of BuNo 58042. Dance was last seen taking to his parachute, but he was subsequently listed as killed in action.

CLARK FIELD COMBAT

On 18 October the fast carriers launched sweeps and strikes against the Philippines in preparation for the Leyte landings. That morning VF-11 put four divisions over land, engaging Japanese Army Air Force fighters overhead Clark Field, northwest of Manila. The fight was resolved wholly in favour of the 'tailhookers', of whom 16 scored 19 victories. John Ramsey splashed two 'Tojos', while Jim Swope got a confirmed and a probable, as did Lt(jg) Clyde Parsley. Swope's section leader, 'Rabbit' Moranville, made his first kill when he downed one of four 'Oscars' claimed by the unit. Lt Henry White splashed a 'Zeke', joining Stimpson, Swope and Ramsey as the only 'Sundowners' to score on both tours. Executive officer Bob Clements claimed a double, raising his tally to three.

Lt Richard F Cyr, a former SBD pilot, was 'belle of the brawl'. It seemed that he had outshot Vern Graham and Charlie Stimpson for the 'Sundowners'' one-day record when he returned with claims for

Hornet plane handlers manoeuvre VF-11 Hellcats on the flightdeck. The officer wearing the leather jacket oversees the operation, supervising the spotting of aircraft. The sailor with the tow bar affixed to No 58's tailwheel has steered the fighter into position while those on the horizontal stabiliser provide the 'horsepower' to move the six-ton Grumman (*via Tailhook Association*)

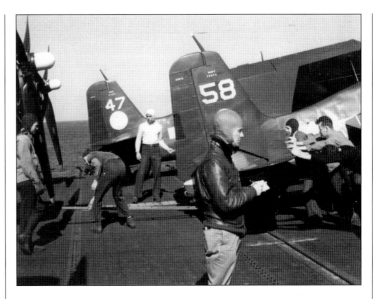

four 'Oscars' and two 'Zekes'. However, subsequent evaluation reduced the figure to four confirmed and two probables. It was a heartbreaker, as Cyr never had another opportunity to score again.

There were more losses that day too, with Ens Warren Derolf last being seen near Manila in BuNo 58839. Then during the dusk recovery Ens George C Anderson's BuNo 58116 crashed into the water. He became was the 11th pilot lost in just nine days.

That evening the 'Sundowners' saw an unusual message on their ready room screen, anticipating an eventful 19th – 'CAPs and VF (fighter) sweeps will be the order of the day until air opposition eliminated. Fighter war tomorrow until air clears. No bombs on or above hangar deck'. However, the expected air battle did not materialise, and carrier pilots only claimed ten shoot-downs in the Manila area throughout the day. The 'Sundowners'' 41 offensive sorties produced no engagements.

Hornet's Task Group 38.1 was near Yap, en route to the anchorage at Ulithi, on 24 October when major elements of the Imperial Japanese Navy appeared in Philippine waters. Rear Adm John S McCain immediately put about and scurried back west, but he was too late to help. CAG-11 missed all the intense action near Leyte Gulf, but at 1030 hrs on the 25th 16 Hellcats and 12 Helldivers were launched 350 nautical miles east of the enemy's reported position. It was one of the longest strikes of the war, but every air group was needed to take advantage of a rare opportunity.

The Japanese force off Samar was one of three that approached Leyte Gulf from the west. Adm Jizaburo Ozawa's carrier force well to the north drew US carriers away from San Bernardino Strait, where Adm Takeo Kurita's powerful surface force hoped to trap American shipping. The Japanese southern group had been destroyed in Surigao Strait during the night of the 24-25 October.

Originally composed of 33 warships, Kurita's centre force had been reduced to four battlewagons, four cruisers and seven destroyers by the morning of the 25th. USS *Intrepid* (CV-11) and USS *Cabot* (CVL-28) air groups had already arrived when *Hornet's* formation sighted the still formidable armada. Strike leader Cdr L A Smith of VB-11 ordered VF-11 down to suppress AA fire while the SB2Cs prepared to attack. The 'Sundowners' pressed through spectacular flak, making repeated runs, only to be frustrated by negligible results. Few bomb hits were made, and TBMs from other air groups suffered extremely poor torpedo performance. Some 'Sundowners' reported that 'tin fish' turned as much as 90 degrees off course or ran too deep.

Follow-up strikes found only one crippled cruiser and a destroyer to finish off, although VF-11 added to its tally later in the day with an 'Oscar' and a 'Tojo'.

Strikes against Japanese fleet units continued for the next two days. Attacking warships near Panay, 'Sundowners' damaged two light cruisers and a destroyer on the 26th – the day the skipper logged his first victory. Fairfax and Ens Howard H Moore each downed an E13A 'Jake' floatplane for the squadron's 49th and 50th kills of the cruise – only five short of the 1943 record.

Fourteen search sorties were flown on the 27th as Adm McCain tried to locate more of the widely-dispersed Japanese fleet, but the VF-11 teams found nothing remarkable. Ens Charles R Bratcres spun in during launch and stood up in his cockpit to signal that he was all right. But after BuNo 70434 sank, a destroyer found only a backpack. Bratcres' harness had probably snagged on the Hellcat's tail when it went down. The next day Task Group 38.1 headed for Ulithi, and a short rest, departing again on 2 November.

Cdr Emmett Riera became CAG-11 after Cdr F R Schrader was killed in October 1944. As one of the few senior officers available, Riera was transferred from command of VB-20 in USS *Enterprise* (CV-6). Though new to *Hornet* (CV-12), he moved in with minimal delay and initially flew the familiar Curtiss SB2C Helldiver. However, as an experienced aviator Riera transitioned to the Hellcat while still at sea and led the air group for the duration of the cruise (*via Tailhook Association*)

That month *Hornet* received a new air group commander, 32-year-old Cdr R E Riera. A Pensacola native, Emmett Riera had graduated well up in the Annapolis class of 1935 and received his wings in January 1940. He already had a Navy Cross as CO of Bombing Squadron 20, but only flew one mission as CAG-11 in an accustomed SB2C before gaining approval from Capt Doyle to check out in the F6F while at sea. From then on Riera flew regularly with VF-11, leading his own division. Furthermore, Emmett Riera was a 'kissing cousin' of Gene Fairfax's wife Juliana.

A new series of strikes was planned for early November but operational losses still mounted. While landing the morning CAP on the 3rd, Ens John J McVeigh spun in and was lost with BuNo

War correspondents and intelligence officers listen to pilots relating events of the recent mission. These men are, from left to right, H E Maring (admin officer, back to camera), A R 'Stubby' Meyers, Blake Moranville, correspondent Keith Wheeler and Jim Swope behind Australian reporter Bill Marien (back to camera) (*via Steve Wells*)

58644. He was the 13th 'Sundowner' to be killed in less than a month, the fourth in an operational accident.

5 November would become the second biggest day in the squadron's long history, and by far the best of the *Hornet* cruise. In two large dogfights around Clark Field, VF-11 shot down 26 aeroplanes for the loss of one Hellcat and pilot in combat. At 0615 hrs Gene Fairfax led 11 F6Fs off *Hornet* as part of a large fighter sweep and eight more as Strike 1A against Clark. In all, Fairfax was leading 87 aircraft from three carriers, including 52 Hellcats from *Hornet*, *Wasp* and USS *Monterey* (CVL-26). The elements of seven squadrons quickly formed up and headed west toward Manila, 160 miles away.

The fighters dispersed and VF-11 shot up eight twin-engined transports on Tarlac Field, but six apparently were badly damaged from earlier attacks and may have been used as decoys. Fairfax then led his divisions south to Mabalacat, where Jim Swope noticed aircraft taking off. Blake Moranville, the aggressive young Nebraskan, tally-hoed a G4M 'Betty' bomber far below, rolled over and made a fast overhead run. He knew that he had hit it solidly but overshot and did not see the result. His wingman, Ens Eddie Kearns, saw the 'Betty' crash.

A large dogfight then broke out as 'Oscars' and 'Tojos' appeared. Moranville pulled up to 4000 ft and got a 'Tojo', but then his guns malfunctioned. He left the hassle to see if he could clear the jams, at which point he spotted a lone Ki-44 fleeing low on the deck. 'I decided I'd better get him before he saw me', Moranville said, and dived behind the Ki-44. 'Rabbit' fired with only one gun operable, but it was enough. The 'Tojo' caught a wingtip on the ground and cartwheeled to destruction.

Meanwhile, the rest of the unit was having a turkey shoot. Fairfax, Swope, Ens Jack M Suddreth, and Lt(jg) Marvin P South all got two 'Tojos', while five others bagged three more Ki-44s and two Ki-43s.

It is uncertain whether this gun camera photo was shot by VF-11, but reputedly it came from 'Sundowner' ace Blake Moranville, who reported an incident in which another Hellcat tried to 'cut in' on a victory (*via Steve Wells*)

VF-11's solitary loss on this occasion was due as much to equipment as to the enemy. Lt William R Sisley was flying an F6F-3 without water injection while his wingman, Ens W M Mann, flew F6F-5P photo-reconnaissance variant BuNo 58199, side number 32. An 'Oscar' attacked Mann, setting his belly tank on fire, and although Sisley turned into the Nakajima in an effort to defend his wingman, he could not get close enough for accurate shooting because his 'dash three' lacked sufficient speed. In desperation Sisley fired at long range, causing the 'Oscar' pilot to break off his attack, but Mann was killed.

Fairfax regrouped the 'Sundowners' and established a CAP over the strike area, then escorted the 35 bombers back to the task force. VF-11 claimed 16 confirmed and two probable victories.

Hornet's Strike 1B had launched at 0900 hrs, and because of the opposition encountered by Fairfax's Strike 1A, it joined up with several Hellcats from *Wasp* for a sweep of Clark Field. The formation arrived over Mt Arayat at about 1015 hrs and, seeing several 'Oscars' below, dived after them. Jimmie Savage related the encounter;

'Several Jap fighters were tally-hoed below and Lt Charlie Stimpson's and my divisions acted as high cover while Lt Cdr Bob Clements and a division from VF-14 off the *Wasp* went down a few thousand feet and engaged them, quickly shooting down four enemy aeroplanes. Things were quiet after that, and Bob came back up to 15,000 ft and joined Charlie and me.

'We milled around awhile before I decided to make a strafing run over the field and see what would happen. Bob and his aeroplanes had gone up north to look over a few small fields, leaving Charlie and me at Clark. My division, composed of Lt(jg) Walter Boring, Lt Daniel T Work and Ens John E Olson, made the first pass, and I was surprised to see AA fire close as I entered the dive. We pulled out at 1000 ft doing some 380 knots.

'Ens Olson, who had just joined my division and was on his first combat mission, reported a Jap aeroplane on his tail. I turned sharply away from Olson to let him pass my position, before turning back toward him and settling down behind the "Oscar". I scared him off Olson with tracers, firing out of range. The Jap turned and twisted, diving for the deck, and I followed, waiting for a good shot. He straightened out momentarily and I settled down dead astern, and just as I started firing a Hellcat came between me and the Jap in an overhead run. It was Olson. I settled down again and put the pipper on the elevator and fired a good long burst. Pieces started coming off the "Oscar" and he flamed immediately, hitting the ground and disintegrating.

'As he flamed I saw another "Oscar" approaching from the port beam. I turned steeply, but Lt(jg) Boring flamed him before I could get in position. As my wingman, he followed me closely. I turned back into a Jap on the starboard beam and he dove for the deck. I fired a few bursts but missed. He cut throttle, and as I overshot with my throttle all the way off, I fired all the way up to his tail, and as I pulled up to miss him he exploded.

'I started for the rally point but was jumped by two more from above. I got a 90-degree shot at one but missed. The other turned away as if to run, and I jumped on his tail and finally shot him down after a chase at treetop level down a road near Clark Field. I again started for the rally point and made a run on another "Oscar" and fired all my ammo without seeing him go down. I quickly turned my and Charlie's division around and headed for home.

'We got ten Jap aeroplanes and nobody was scratched. Besides Lt Cdr Clements' two, I got three, Lt Work two, Lt Stimpson three and Ens W H Boring a probable. The day's score for VF-11 was 26-to-1 – much better than at Formosa. We were getting experience and confidence.'

The only other loss of the day came at noon when Ens Matthew Crehan, waiting to land aboard, had to ditch astern of the ship (probably in BuNo 58981). He was rescued by the destroyer USS *Blue* (DD-744), mindful that four other *Hornet* fighter plots had been lost in similar circumstances.

Sweeps and strikes continued for the next two weeks but relatively little air combat resulted. The 'Sundowners' splashed three snoopers on 13 November, although two 'Oscars' bounced Swope's division while escorting Cdr Riera and badly shot up Ens Charles E Boineau's F6F – he landed without the use of his flaps. Charlie Stimpson made his last two kills on the 14th with a 'Zeke' and a 'Tony', and he was the only pilot to score that day.

Strike 1C, launched at noon on the 14th, put 27 'Sundowners' over enemy airfields in company with *Enterprise's* VF-20. Returning pilots

CAG-11 prepares to launch a strike in late 1944. Nine F6F-5s (most armed with HVARs) are turning up ahead of eight TBM-3s and nine SB2C-3s. Aside from the white ball on the vertical stabiliser, *Hornet* **Hellcats and Avengers sported white propeller hubs to enhance recognition in flight (***via Tailhook Association***)**

counted 40 to 50 burning aircraft at Del Carmen and about 15 at Porlac. *Hornet* sent the congratulatory message 'Fighter(s) enjoyed working with *Enterprise*'. The 'Big E's' CAG replied, '99 *Enterprise* very appreciative of the compliment. Particularly so since the pilots who paid the compliment produced so splendidly on today's sweep'.

That day 'Rabbit' Moranville became the sixth 'Sundowner' ace when he bagged a Ki-46 'Dinah', while Ens Joseph V Pavela got a 'Betty'.

In strikes against Subic Bay on 19 November, Fairfax's initial strafing run caused explosions aboard an estimated 4000-ton cargo ship. Other Hellcats pressed home the attack, sinking the vessel – possibly the 3700-ton *Seian Maru*.

During the noon recovery Lt Oscar H West Jr put 'Fox 31' (BuNo 42639) in the water near the task force. His wingman, Ens Jerry Coeur, circled the splash until a ship arrived, then Coeur diverted to USS *Cowpens* (CVL-25), refuelled, and returned to *Hornet* two hours later. That evening, nightfighter pilot Ens Robert Witzig drifted to starboard in the groove and crashed over the side in BuNo 58352. Fortunately, a destroyer was able to find him in the darkness and fetch him back.

Bob Saggau, the former All-American athlete, diverted to Tacloban airfield due to a worrisome oil pressure reading after an anti-shipping strike on 10 November. 'As MacArthur had just landed on Leyte, I thought I might have the chance to tell him what the *real* war was about', Saggau quipped. But the only person he talked to was the GI jeep driver who led him to the parking area. It turned out that both men were from the same county in Iowa.

On 20 November *Hornet's* task group prepared to return to Ulithi, but 26 junior pilots were transferred to other carriers, along with their aircraft. Although some of them eventually rejoined VF-11, their departure came as a shock to the squadron. Indeed, Gene Fairfax looked upon it as the loss of a large part of his family.

The 'Sundowners' enjoyed an unusually lengthy rest while the task group laid up at Ulithi late that month. Other than two test hops, almost no flying was done between 23-30 November. Some local CAPs were conducted during the first week in December, leading up to the next sortie on the 10th. That afternoon the 'Sundowners' launched 47 Hellcats in two 'group gropes' to practice for upcoming operations in the Philippines.

Meanwhile, 'Fighting 11's' pilot strength was doubled as a matter of policy. After the appearance of kamikazes in the Philippines, increased demands on fighter squadrons resulted in authorised strength being

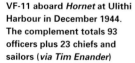

VF-11 aboard *Hornet* at Ulithi Harbour in December 1944. The complement totals 93 officers plus 23 chiefs and sailors (*via Tim Enander*)

established at no fewer than 105 pilots and about 75 aircraft. Consequently, in early December the 'Sundowners' received two more lieutenant commanders – Fritz E Wolf and Edward H Bayers. Wolf was a veteran of the American Volunteer Group in China in 1941-42, where he had been credited with 2.5 confirmed victories. Bayers, who had 2.333 victories to his name following a combat tour with *Enterprise's* VF-6 in 1942, was an old friend of Bob Clements, who described him as 'the best fighter pilot I ever knew'.

Clements might have obtained his own command at that time, as some air groups were dividing their enlarged fighter squadrons into two units, with one designated a fighter-bomber outfit. Emmett Riera and Gene Fairfax discussed the situation and decided there was no need to change – Clements agreed. With more missions to be flown, the workload remained the same for each division, and administration proved no major problem.

The fast carriers briefly returned to the Philippines, where a series of strikes was flown between 13-16 December. Four more victories were added to VF-11's total during this period, making 87 to date for the WestPac deployment.

Squadron and aircraft records appear contradictory during this period, for as many as five Hellcats were lost on the 14th, including Lt W D Zoecklein's BuNo 58660, which was safely ditched. However, the daily operations summary mentions no losses in 129 sorties. Deck crashes possibly accounted for the other losses. The 15th began poorly when Ens W E Lizotte's BuNo 70557 suffered engine failure on launch. 'Lizzy' had no option except to ditch 'Fox 14', but a destroyer quickly retrieved him. Meanwhile, Jimmie Savage continued his rare status as a photo-reconnaissance ace;

'Took off on a photo and escort mission. Target was Del Carmen Field, south of Clark. We approached at 13,000 ft with no opposition

The strain of continuous combat operations shows on the face of **Lt Wesley E Lizotte**, still wearing flight gear in the ready room. He was credited with two 'Oscars' destroyed during the deployment. An unidentified replacement pilot stands behind him (*via Steve Wells*)

Hornet fighter pilots man aircraft in December 1944. Those identified are (from left to right) Swope, Stimpson, two unknown pilots, Wolf and Moranville. Lt Cdr Fritz E Wolf, formerly of the 'Flying Tigers', briefly flew with VF-11 before joining VBF-3 in *Yorktown* (CV-10) in February 1945 (*via Tailhook Association*)

except AA. I made my photo runs as our VB and VT did the bombing. After I had taken the required pictures, I made a rocket run on some parked aeroplanes and pulled out toward the rally point. I heard a "tally-ho", and upon looking down I spotted a "Judy" low and 45 degrees to my port side. I swung around and gave full throttle to catch him but Lt A J Meyer was already shooting at him. I throttled back, and as Meyer overran him, I closed to 900 ft and opened fire. He took evasive action by turning and slipping, and the pilot threw out a parachute, which passed just under my wing. I flamed him then at about 50 ft off the deck, and as he exploded on the ground a wheel came up higher than my aeroplane.

'We reformed our flight and returned to the *Hornet* after searching the east coast for a downed pilot.'

In two days of operations over Subic Bay VF-11 beached and burned out a 7000-ton transport, five pilots, including Lt Cdr Bayers, claiming bomb and rocket hits on *Oryoku Maru* – one of the most notorious 'hell ships' transporting Allied prisoners to Japan. In the same period CAG Riera's division claimed to have sunk a destroyer escort, while Ens Robcke and Ens Bilbao blew up a 3000-ton cargo vessel.

Flight operations ceased completely on 17 December, and remained badly affected the following day, due to the onset of Typhoon 'Cobra'. During the height of the storm two destroyers astern of *Hornet* rolled over and sank. Search missions were flown for crippled ships en route back to Ulithi, where the task force spent the holidays.

At year-end the forward-deployed *Essex* class carriers averaged 51 fighters apiece, which matched VF-11's inventory exactly (including 36 F6F-5s and -5Ns). But even amid the kamikaze crisis, big-deck carriers still embarked about 24 dive-bombers and 18 torpedo-bombers. That would shortly change as fighting-bombing squadrons were added to the task force.

THE NEW YEAR

Hornet exercised its aircraft in predawn operations on 1 January 1945, then headed west to the now-familiar hunting grounds of Formosa.

Lt Jim Swope holds the brakes of 'Ginger 29' in response to a plane director's raised fist as *Hornet* prepares to launch fighters. Absence of HVARs indicates that the mission was probably a combat air patrol (*via Tailhook Asociation*)

In a predawn mission on the 3rd, Gene Fairfax was leading two divisions against Tainan when he spotted a H6K 'Mavis' flying-boat flying low over the water, providing antisubmarine protection for a convoy. Fairfax and his wingman, Jack 'Soapy' Suddreth, both attacked unsuccessfully, before Jim Swope's fire caused it to explode. Later that day VF-11 damaged a transport ship and an oiler.

By 6 January the task force was back in the Philippines, with sweeps over Mabalacat and Bambam airfields. Lt Dan Work's division clamed two 'Zekes' shot down and two probables, raising the 'Sundowners'' *Hornet* total to 90 destroyed in the air.

The next day brought more combat over the same area, during which Lt(jg) John Sims in BuNo 71941 lost formation in some heavy clouds and was never seen again. The second of the morning's strikes encountered 'Zekes' and 'Tojos', with Henry White claiming two of the latter to become the last 'Sundowner' ace. Ens Jack H Robcke also bagged a 'Zeke', but Ens James H Bethel Jr was killed in

Ordnancemen prepare to load a 500-lb general purpose bomb on 'Ginger 13', one of VF-11's F6F-5s. Hellcats frequently flew strike missions with bombs and/or HVARs, compensating for the reduced number of SB2Cs and TBMs embarked during the kamikaze crisis of late 1944. Note that 'Ginger 56' was a replacement aircraft, bearing a horizontal stripe that was painted over following its transfer to *Hornet* (*via Tailhook Association*)

BuNo 71904 when he tried to follow a 'Zeke' in a split-S from 800 ft. Other pilots reported that Bethel had not even reached the vertical when his Hellcat hit the water. Later, BuNo 58594 was lost when Lt(jg) M J Hayter ran out of fuel, but he was rescued.

That evening *Hornet* copied a message from CTF-38 that attested to the proficiency gained in months of operations. Vice Adm John S McCain sent to Rear Adm Gerald F Bogan of TG-38.2, 'Will you compliment your group on your excellent rendezvous this morning. There were practically no transmissions, and your pilots deserve a "well done". Nice work'.

Meanwhile, the US Sixth Army prepared to land at Lingayen Gulf on Luzon's west coast, evoking a severe response from the Japanese. A renewed kamikaze offensive prompted the commander of the Third Fleet to issue the following directive;

'Luzon is now a bloody battleground. The enemy is fighting to the death to destroy our expeditionary forces and kill the embarked American soldiers. Many ships have been hard hit in the past two days. Every undestroyed enemy aeroplane is a potential threat to our comrades and a threat to its success. This is the time for great effort and great determination. Give it your best and God bless you. Halsey.'

Yet another operational loss occurred on launch on the morning of the 8th when Ens P E King's engine suffered a catastrophic failure – a rarity for the rugged Pratt & Whitney R-2800 that powered the F6F Hellcat – and he crashed spectacularly in 'Fox 18'. BuNo 42294 exploded on impact with the water, but somehow King emerged unharmed.

On 9 January the 'Sundowners' were back over Formosa for a highly successful anti-shipping strike. Cdr Riera led a division that sank a 'destroyer escort', while Lt Cdr Ed Bayers' division was largely responsible for the destruction of another 'destroyer'. A 10,000-ton oiler and a 3000-ton transport were also sunk by bombs and rockets, while three more ships of 16,000 gross tons were damaged.

During the night of 11-12 January, TF-38 entered the South China Sea for the first carrier attack against French Indochina. Fairfax's pilots flew four strikes, two sweeps, seven CAPs and two photo-missions on the 12th – 133 sorties in all. Two small escorts were claimed sunk in

Three of VF-11's aces grab a snack in the galley adjoining the ready room. Jim Swope conducts a post mortem while Charlie Stimpson and Blake Moranville look on. The latter pilot was shot down while strafing near Saigon, French Indochina, on 12 January 1945. Briefly held by the Vichy French, he made his way to safety in Kunming, China, after becoming one of only two US Navy ace PoWs. The other, VF-15's Ens Kenneth Flinn, died of malnutrition in Japanese hands (*via Tailhook Association*)

Cam Ranh Bay, one by the proficient team of Ed Bayers and Ens Frank C Onion Jr, while five destroyers and two transports were damaged.

No enemy aircraft were encountered by the 'Sundowners', but for the first and last time a VF-11 ace was lost in combat. On the second sweep Jim Swope's division was strafing and rocketing Saigon's Tan Son Nhut airport when 'Rabbit' Moranville's F6F was hit by ground fire. Although he had once brought a badly shot-up F6F back to *Hornet* and broke his arresting hook on landing, this time Moranville knew the Pratt & Whitney would burn itself out in a few minutes. He had no choice but to look for a landing spot.

Heading southwest, Swope and his wingmates escorted Moranville to the southern part of the Mekong Delta. Oil pressure in the stricken Hellcat was almost zero by then, with the engine temperature well into the red. Abruptly the R-2800 seized tight, the three-bladed propeller wrenching to a halt. Moranville spotted a large rice paddy on the north bank of the Song Hau River and turned to set up his approach. With the canopy locked back, magneto switched off, fuel off and his shoulder harness extra tight, the 21-year-old ace reached to his left and dropped his arresting hook. When he got down to the last few feet it would drag along the surface, telling him that he was close enough to stall the aeroplane in. Moranville had a good long approach, allowing ample time to set up his glide angle.

Deciding to keep the flaps up until he cleared the near row of trees, the ace noticed a large number of people standing on the dikes surrounding the paddy and he assumed that they were peasants. Then he was concentrating on his landing.

When he cleared the trees, Moranville dropped the flaps and kept milking the control column back as the blunt nose came up. He felt the hook grabbing at the water. That was it. He brought the control column clear back and the Hellcat splashed down smoothly. Moranville did not know it, but he was 75 miles southwest of Saigon, between the villages of Tra On and Cau Ke.

'Rabbit' flipped the IFF destruct switch on the electrical panel to prevent the Japanese from learning the transponder's frequency should they find 'Ginger 30'. Then he unbuckled his seat belt and shoulder harness and stood up in the cockpit. He knew that Swope and the others were still overhead, but paid them little attention. With his parachute still strapped on, he climbed out and stepped from the wing into knee-deep water. He sloshed past the Hellcat's nose, and although he did not stop to look closely, Moranville saw that small arms fire had struck the prop governor. Otherwise he saw little damage except for one wingtip slightly dented from the landing. Moranville did not learn about the 20 mm hole in the cowling until years later, as it was hidden below water.

Still circling, Jim Swope was keeping an eye on the downed aeroplane and pilot. 'Blake was a lonely looking figure, standing in the rice paddy by his aeroplane', Swope said, 'and all three of us would have landed alongside him if we had thought it would help'. But that was impossible, so they did the next best thing to help their friend. Swope opened his canopy and tossed out his emergency packet of money – Bank of Shanghai gold notes – in the hope that Moranville could use it. Eddie Kearns and Charlie Boineau did the same, but Moranville never saw the packets falling into the paddy. After a few more moments the three F6Fs set course back to *Hornet*.

Moranville turned and started walking toward the edge of the paddy, wondering what he was going to do next. It was rough going with the parachute still strapped on – he almost slapped his head. He had not unclipped his parachute pack as part of the ditching procedure. He slogged back to the aeroplane, took off the parachute and laid it carefully on the wing. Aviators were taught from primary training onward that parachutes were lifesaving devices, and should be treated as such. Moranville had just set his pack down, keeping the straps from dangling in the water, when he stood upright and almost shouted aloud, 'What am I doing?' Obviously the parachute was no longer important – he was wasting precious time. He considered burning the Hellcat to deprive the Japanese of it, but decided he should get out of the area immediately.

Angry with himself about the parachute ('I had other things on my mind'), Moranville crossed the paddy, climbed an embankment and started walking, not knowing where he wanted to go. He had a vague notion that if he could get to the Philippines he would be all right. Then suddenly he was surrounded by people atop the dike. He considered reaching for the 0.38-cal revolver under his left arm but recognised the people as Annamites. They were obviously the same ones he had seen during his final moments in the air.

James S Swope was a private pilot before winning his US Navy wings in 1942. He became a '92 percent ace' flying with VF-11 at Guadalcanal, and added five more victories embarked in *Hornet*. A career aviator, Swope commanded a fighter squadron and a carrier air group before retiring in 1967. Subsequently he entered the perfume business and died in his native Texas in 2000 (*via Tailhook Association*)

Moranville stared at them for a minute and they stared back. Not knowing what else to do, he began speaking slowly, asking for assistance but getting no response. He tried a few more times before he heard a small boy say something in English.

Moranville concentrated on the boy, who proved reluctant to talk but eventually admitted that he spoke broken English. Following more lengthy discourse, the lad and an old man agreed to lead the American to safety. They took him to a peasant house and gave him a bottle of soda water before continuing. After another hour's walk they neared a small village and Moranville pulled up short. He suspected a trap, figuring he was being delivered to the Japanese. But he had nowhere else to go, and as a precaution he unsnapped the strap over his revolver. The boy saw the movement and shook his head. 'No, no. No worry'. Moranville nodded and they continued on, but the pilot remained wary. 'If these characters are leading me into a trap', he thought, 'the Japs may get me but I'll get these two'.

The boy and the old man took Moranville to the village church and then left. Many villagers came by to look at the stranger but did not bother him. As it was nearly dark, Moranville settled down to try to sleep but could not doze off. He had been there about 90 minutes when he heard a car drive up and, tense and alert, he saw a white man in civilian clothes enter the church.

'I am French', the man said, explaining in fairly fluent English that he was magistrate of the area, and provided some cognac. He had come to take 'le aviateur Americaine' to safety, if 'Lt Moranville' would care to step into the vehicle parked outside. Once again things seemed to be decided for him so Moranville went to the Frenchman's car, a coal-burning automobile. It was the first the American had ever seen, and the official explained that gasoline was in short supply in Indochina. 'The war, you know'.

Thus began Blake Moranville's two-and-a-half-month saga of escape and evasion in French Indochina. Sheltered by both the native population and the French colonial administration from occupying Japanese forces, Moranville was spirited from one location to another, finally participating with the French Foreign Legion in a fighting retreat to Dien Bien Phu on the Laotian border. With six other American airmen, he was eventually airlifted out of Vietnam by US Army Intelligence and units of the Fourteenth Air Force as Japanese forces closed in on Dien Bien Phu.

On the day that Moranville went down, concern was somewhat alleviated by the fact that 'Rabbit' was seen walking around his aeroplane, and five days later *Hornet* received word that he was with the French. But 'Gunner' the mascot was despondent over the loss of his master. Happily, they were reunited several months later in Nebraska. When the aviator returned home he found that '"Gunner" was my dad's dog'.

FORMOSA, HONG KONG AND OKINAWA

Near Hainan Island on 14 January, the search team of Lt J S Welfelt and Ens H J Stockert found a 2000-ton cargo ship. They attacked with rockets, following with strafing passes that left the vessel 'sinking'.

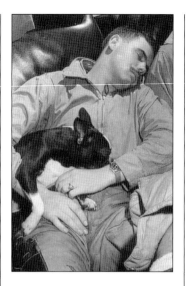

Twenty-year-old H B Moranville received his US Navy wings in July 1943 and joined VF-11 as its junior pilot. Nicknamed 'Rabbit' (for the similar surname he shared with a famous baseball player), he was assigned to care for the squadron mascot, 'Gunner'. They were inseparable until then-Lt(jg) Moranville was shot down over Indochina in January 1945. They were reunited after the war (*via Henk van der Lugt*)

On the morning of the 15th TF-38 again launched sweeps against Formosa, while Gene Fairfax took two of his own divisions and four from other squadrons for a look at Hong Kong. About 50 miles east of the target area Fairfax noticed a L2D 'Tabby' transport (a Japanese-built DC-3). The presence of four 'Zeke' escorts indicated an important passenger aboard the Nakajima, and the CO radioed to 'Leave the transport aeroplane until we have the escorts'. Fairfax, Jake Robcke, Ens Howard H Moore and James P Wolf each got a 'Zeke', then Fairfax and 'Soapy' Suddreth went after the 'Tabby'. 'We probably overkilled it', Fairfax said, and the only way to decide credit was to flip a coin. It was squadron policy not to split a kill, and Suddreth won the toss. The 'Tabby' went in the records as his third victory – Fairfax now had four.

In 1976 Professor Alvin Coox determined that the transport's VIP passenger was Vice Adm Kouichiro Hatakeyama, who was in the process of inspecting Japanese defences in southern China when his transport was downed. Hatakeyama had ordered the murder of 300 Allied PoWs in the East Indies in 1942.

The only other aerial victory on the 15th was a B6N 'Jill' torpedo-bomber downed by Swope for his fifth kill of the tour, and last of the war.

Next day the squadron was back over Hong Kong in force, suffering two losses from 54 sweep and strike sorties. A 10,000-ton oiler was severely damaged by an estimated 12 rocket hits, while Stimpson's division set afire the oil storage area and 'Cac' Flath's pilots worked over Kowloon Docks. Ens Matt Crehan's BuNo 71082 was damaged by flak over the harbour on Strike 1C and he bailed out near Tamkan Island while his division leader, Bob Clements, circled overhead.

With no other Hellcats in the area, Clements radioed a bomber pilot who dropped a life raft, as Crehan's had drifted away. The replacement failed to inflate, however, so Clements somehow managed to drop his own and Crehan climbed in. Calling for a rescue submarine, the executive officer scared away fishing boats and sampans until his ammunition ran out, only to discover that the submarine could not go close enough to shore. The conscientious 'XO' remained until his radio quit and he had 30 gallons of fuel remaining. He sweated all the way back to *Hornet*, landing with the gauge reading empty.

Crehan was not found by subsequent searches, and he appeared in the squadron cruise book among those killed in action. Not until after the war did Clements learn from Crehan himself that the youngster had been fished from the water by friendly Chinese who then helped him get to Kunming, where he met Blake Moranville! World War 2 could become surprisingly small.

It was still a shooting war, however, and Ens Richard Wilson's BuNo 70561 fell to AA fire during Strike 1D. He was the 17th, and last, 'Sundowner' killed during the deployment.

After Hong Kong it was back to Formosa on 21 January, where VF-11 damaged five auxiliary ships totalling 25,000 tons, plus two destroyers. In the squadron's final dogfight Lt William R Sisley led his division into a formation of 'Zekes' and 'Judys'. Sisley and Lt(jg) Thomas S Williams each claimed a 'Zeke', while Ens Zebulon V Knott

VF-11's ready room near the end of the *Hornet* cruise. In the front row, from left to right, are 'Doc' Savage, Bill Eccles with 'Gunner', 'exec' Bob Clements and possibly J S Sims. Second row, unknown, Sol White, (aisle) Jim Swope and unknown. Behind Swope are Stimpson and Jack Welfelt. Playing cards in the rear are Wes Lizotte, John Willis and Jerry Coeur (*via Steve Wells*)

downed a 'Judy' and Ens Robert McReynolds was credited with a probable 'Zeke'. One more Hellcat was lost when Lt Cdr Fritz Wolf splashed down after launch with zero oil pressure in 'Fox 49' (BuNo 41517), but he was rescued by a destroyer. The next day VF-11 flew its last combat missions of the war in sweeps and strikes over Okinawa.

The squadron's final sorties garnered some national coverage from Keith Wheeler, a veteran correspondent for *The Chicago Daily Times*. Riding *Hornet*, he was impressed with the story of two 'Sundowners'' encounter with a sharp-shooting Okinawan farmer;

'Anybody who comes from North Dakota as I do knows that North Dakotans are slow to anger but terrible when aroused.

'Two North Dakotans are twice as terrible.

'This is about two Philosophical North Dakotans who lost their tempers and took a terrible vengeance.

'Lt Robert ("Cactus") Flath, 25, of Stanley, North Dakota, flies lead man of a fighter division. Ens Paul Warren, 21, of Parshall, North Dakota, leads the division second section.

'Another thing I forgot to mention about North Dakotans is that they don't generally talk much, possibly because in North Dakota there is seldom anyone in range of your voice. "Cactus" and Paul flew together for two months before either knew they were born within 40 miles of one another.

'It took another two months for them to learn that the Warrens of Parshall have for years consulted a Stanley dentist who just happens to be "Cactus's" uncle.

VF-11 Hellcats return to *Hornet* during operations in February 1945. The squadron's final mission was flown against Okinawa early that month (*via Steve Wells*)

'Well the other day "Cactus" took his division over Okinawa Jima, an island about 250 miles from the Jap homeland. Paul, as customary, had the second section.

'Targets were scarce that day. No shipping appeared. The Japs appeared to have run out of aeroplanes. So "Cactus" led his division down a snaky little railroad and they chased along it at 20 ft looking for a train to strafe or, failing that, a section hand's push car.

'They followed the rails ten miles and hadn't turned up even a track walker. They were nearing Naha Town and their altitude of almost nothing was a little too skimpy for the locality, as Naha's anti-aircraft is plentiful and pretty sharp. "Cactus" decided to pull the division up and out. He banked sharply, roaring away from the tracks and beginning to climb. Paul's section heeled over and followed through as though all four aeroplanes were wired together.

'As they ripped across a rice paddy "Cactus" saw out of the corner of his eye a farmer standing a few feet below. Straw hatted, overalled and barefooted, the farmer stared up and "Cactus" thought he shook his fist.

'He had flashed from sight when "Cactus" heard a sharp "splat" and saw a small hole come through his fuselage. Seconds later Paul called him by radio.

"The goddam clodhopper hit me!"

'"Whaddya mean clodhopper? Who hit you? Where?"' Cactus answered.

'"That farmer. Didn't ya see him? He had his old gopher rifle and hit me. Splattered glass in my face – the doggone independent operator", Paul yelled.

'"Hit me too", Cactus said. "What's he think he is, anti-aircraft? Where's his union card?" Cactus howled.

'And so the two outraged North Dakotans went back and burned the farmer's barn, scared his chickens out of a month's production and strafed his chick sale.'

In their last action, on 22 January, the 'Sundowners' mauled a cargo ship, possibly the 2073-ton *Hikosan Maru*, which sank.

At month-end VF-11 had a full allotment of 73 aircraft, including 13 F6F-3s. By then the old model Hellcat was a rarity, as most air groups had been fully equipped with 'dash fives'.

SUMMARY

From 10 October 1944 to 22 January1945 the 'Sundowners' were credited with 103 Japanese aircraft shot down and 16 probables, in addition to 288 claimed on the ground. A destroyer and three escorts were credited to the unit as being sunk, with 21 similar vessels damaged to varying extents. Five cargo ships, transports and oilers totalling 27,000 tons were reckoned sunk by Fairfax's Hellcats and nearly 180,000 tons damaged.

Pilot losses amounted to 20, including Cdr Schrader who was killed, and Moranville and Crehan who safely returned to the US. Of those, the seven lost in air combat represented the single largest cause, while five were killed by anti-aircraft fire. Two pilots were lost to unknown causes but both were believed inflicted by enemy action – DeRolf near Manila and Sims over Luzon.

Excluding aircraft damaged beyond local repair, VF-11 lost 27 F6Fs, including 12 to operational causes. Eight were downed by AA fire and seven in aerial combat. The 'Sundowner' Hellcats lost in aerial combat resulted in a kill-loss ratio of nearly 15-to-1. Additionally, the *Hornet* nightfighter detachment lost a pilot and two aircraft in accidents, but those casualties were not attributed to VF-11.

Hornet and its squadrons were awarded the Presidential Unit Citation for actions during VF-11's deployment.

The 103 victories scored under Fairfax established VF-11 as the 17th ranked Hellcat squadron among more than 80 that flew F6Fs in combat. One fact that Fairfax's pilots were especially proud of was that no CAG-11 dive-bomber or torpedo-bomber was lost to enemy aircraft.

This end-of-cruise PR photo showed the 'Sundowners'' 'top guns', Charlie Stimpson in the cockpit and Jim Swope on the port wing. Both scored on each tour, finishing with 16 and 9.66 victories, respectively. The much-adorned F6F-3 was obviously decorated for publicity purposes, showing Stimpson's ultimate score with the squadron emblem. Its side number was probably 16 (*via Tailhook Association*)

Score

Enemy planes destroyed in the air   -   - 102
Enemy planes probably destroyed in the air -   18
Enemy planes destroyed-damaged on ground - 567
Warships Sunk: 1 Destroyer, 3 Destroyer Escorts
Warships Damaged: 1 Heavy Cruiser, 2 Light
  Cruisers, 16 Destroyers, 5 Destroyer Escorts, 1
  Destroyer Tender.
Merchant Shipping Sunk: -   -   27,350 Tons
Merchant Shipping Damaged: - 178,900 Tons
Total Shipping Sunk or Damaged: 285,000 Tons
Destroyed: 25 Locomotives, 47 Trucks, 43 Barges,
  3 Oil Dumps.
Strikes: 134. Combat Hrs.: 14,125. Sorties: 1428.

Fighting Squadron Eleven

1944   1945

Strike Record
USS HORNET

1944 Oct. 10 - Nansei Shoto: Okinawa shipping and airfields. **Oct. 11 -** Philippines: Manila Bay shipping and Luzon airfields. **Oct. 12 - 16 -** Formosa: Takao Harbor shipping, southern Formosa airfields, and Task Group protection from enemy air attacks. **Oct. 18 - 19 -** Philippines: Luzon airfields. **Oct. 20 -** Philippines: Air support for Leyte invasion. **Oct. 25 - 26 -** 2nd Battle of the Philippine Sea off Leyte Gulf. **Nov. 5 - 6 -** Philippines: Luzon airfields. **Nov. 11 -** Attack on enemy, Leyte bound troop convoy. **Nov. 13 - 14 -** Philippines: Manila Bay shipping. **Nov. 19 -** Philippines: Luzon airfields. **Nov. 21 -** Yap Island airfields. **Dec. 14 - 16 -** Philippines: Luzon airfields in support of Mindoro Invasion. **1945 Jan. 3 - 4 -** Formosa and Pescadores Is.: Shipping and Tainan airfields. **Jan. 6 - 7 -** Philippines: Luzon airfields. **Jan. 9 -** Formosa: Tainan airfields in support of Luzon Invasion. **Jan. 12 -** French Indo China: Saigon airfields and attack on two enemy convoys off Camranh Bay. **Jan. 15 -** Formosa: Pescadores Is. shipping. **Jan. 16 -** China: Hong Kong shipping and airfields. **Jan. 21 -** Formosa: Takao shipping and airfields. **Jan. 22 -** Nansei Shoto: Okinawa airfields.

Lt. Comdr. Eugene G. Fairfax, USN, Comdg. Fighting Squadron Eleven.

From 1943 to 1945 VF-11's 157 victories ranked its 11th among all US Navy squadrons, with 11 pilots and 17 Grummans lost in aerial combat. Charlie Stimpson set the pace on both tours with a total of 16 destroyed, followed by Jim Swope with 10. Then came 'Doc' Savage with seven, Blake Moranville with six and Bob Clements, Vern Graham and Henry White with five each. The seven aces had accounted for 54 victories, or more than one-third of the total. 'Sundowners' had downed 15 different types of Japanese aircraft, including 120 fighters.

In late February CAG-11 arrived at NAS Alameda, California, where it remained through April. The 'Sundowners' spent June and July training at Naval Auxiliary Air Station (NAAS) Fallon, Nevada, before rejoining the air group at NAAS Santa Rosa, north of San Francisco.

Meanwhile, in April 1945 Fairfax had departed for NAS Los Alamitos, California, when he assumed command of VF-98, the West Coast fighter training squadron. He took Jim Swope with him, while 'Doc' Savage went to VBF-98. Blake Moranville rejoined VF-11 briefly at NAAS Fallon for a boisterous three-day reunion in Reno and finished the war as an instrument instructor. Bob Clements returned to the Naval Academy.

With Fairfax's departure Lt George M Bert became interim CO until the arrival of Lt Cdr Percival W Jackson, who remained into the postwar period. When Japan's delegates signed the surrender documents on 2 September the 'Sundowners' were still at Santa Rosa, preparing to deploy for the invasion of Japan, scheduled for

At the end of the *Hornet* deployment VF-11 produced this bi-fold 'business card' printed with the unit's 1944-45 record for the use of all squadron personnel (*Steve Wells*)

Upon its return from the Pacific in February 1945, CAG-11 began 'turnaround training' at NAAS Santa Rosa, California, preparing for a third deployment. VF-11's F6F-5s were marked with 'M' prefixes on the fuselage and lower port wing during this period. The '311' on the nose of the second Hellcat indicates that it was recently arrived, retaining its ferry or delivery number (*via Tailhook Association*)

1 November. At that time the air group's complement was 68 Hellcats, 15 Avengers, and 15 Helldivers.

POSTWAR

Adjusting to the dramatic force reduction after 1945 affected every unit in the US Navy. However, VF-11 continued training, with carrier qualifications aboard two escort carriers in August and December. Then in February 1946 CAG-11 deployed to Hawaii for eight months, flying from USS *Lexington* (CV-16) and USS *Shangri-La* (CV-38).

When Percival Jackson rolled out in May 1946, Gene Fairfax returned for a rare second command tour with the same squadron. He recalled, 'I was offered a choice between an F8F squadron that was heading out and VF-11 that was training in Hawaii. I chose "Fighting

This F6F-5 suffered an in flight engine failure during 'turnaround training' on 7 May 1945, causing its pilot to hastily belly land on the range at NAF Fallon (*via Henk van der Lugt*)

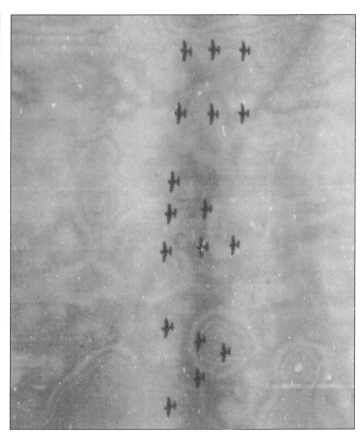

Eleven 'Sundowner' Hellcats appropriately spell the squadron designation in this formation fly-by from 1945 (*Henk van der Lugt via Tailhook Association*)

11" again because there were still guys there that I knew, and of course I liked the squadron'. Fairfax was relieved by Cdr Howard W Crews in September. The latter was a veteran of the 'Cactus Air Force', having scored two victories at Guadalcanal while flying F4Fs with VF-5.

In November 1946, shortly after VF-11 returned to San Diego from Hawaii, the squadron identity changed. In a US Navy-wide redesignation of aviation units, VF-11 became VF-11A. The air group's other squadrons became VF-12A, VA-11A and VA-12A. However, the system proved ill conceived, and was replaced in less than two years.

Between December 1946 and December 1949 the 'Sundowners' flew their third consecutive Grumman fighter in the form of the spectacular F8F Bearcat. Carrier operations were conducted irregularly in the postwar era of severe budget cuts.

Lt Cdr Robert S Merritt served as acting skipper during June and July 1947 until Cdr Richard S Rogers reported aboard in time to prepare the 'Sundowners' for their first world cruise. Hailing from Texas, Rogers was an unusually experienced aviator. Following graduation from Annapolis in 1937, he served as ship's company before earning his wings in 1940. Over the next five years he served in VF-3, VS-201, and two composite squadrons. Rogers flew antisubmarine missions with VC-9 in USS *Bogue* (CVE-9) and survived the 'Battle of the Taffies' with VC-68 in USS *Fanshaw Bay* (CVE-70). CAG-11 was Cdr R L Fowler, who had led VC-5 from USS *Fanshaw Bay* (CVE-71) in the same engagement.

Redesignated VF-11A in November 1946, the squadron exchanged its F6F-5s for F8F-1s at year end. Thus, the 'Sundowners' flew Bearcats during the *Valley Forge* world cruise from October 1947 to June 1948. The unit designation was changed to VF-111 a month later (*via Henk van der Lugt*)

CAG-11's commemorative patch for *Valley Forge's* world cruise, whuch ran from October 1947 through to June 1948 (*via Tailhook Association*)

CAG-11 prepares for a deckload launch from *Valley Forge* probably during its 1947-48 world cruise. The F8F-1s with the 100-series side numbers belong to the 'Sundowners', then designated VF-11A, while the 200 series machines are from VF-12A, which became VF-112 in July of 1948 (*Steve Wells*)

During the autumn of 1947 CAG-11 was paired with its new aircraft carrier in San Diego. USS *Valley Forge* (CV-45) had been built partly with wartime funds donated by citizens of Philadelphia, Pennsylvania, and after it was commissioned in November 1946 the vessel conducted a Caribbean shakedown with CAG-5 from January to March 1947, before proceeding to San Diego in August.

After embarking the air group, 'Happy Valley' steamed westward in October, spending three months training in Hawaiian waters en route to the Western Pacific. CAG-11's two fighter squadrons flew F8F-1s while its attack squadrons retained SB2C-5 Helldivers and TBM-3 Avengers. Riding *Valley Forge* was Rear Adm Harold M Martin, sardonically nicknamed 'Beauty' by his Annapolis classmates, Class of 1919. His TF-38 included four destroyers and an oiler, which he took to Australia and Hong Kong. On 1 March, having departed the China coast, the group was ordered to return via the Atlantic, turning the deployment into a world cruise. Thus the carrier and its escorts made the grand tour, including the Philippines, Singapore, Ceylon and the Persian Gulf.

In late March *Valley Forge* hosted the Saudi crown prince's retinue, which had been invited to observe carrier operations. However, a sand storm limited the display to two Bearcats. Subsequently, 'Happy Valley' and its escorts transited the Suez Canal, CV-45 reportedly being the largest carrier yet to ply that waterway. From there it steamed for Gibraltar and points north.

In late April *Valley Forge* squirmed through potentially dangerous Norwegian fjords, where snow limited visibility to barely 30 yards. Nevertheless, the carrier moored in Bergen's crowded harbour and

A division of VF-11A aircraft, probably over Hawaii. The V tail code signifies *Valley Forge* to which CAG-11 was assigned in 1947-48 (*Steve Wells*)

prepared to join in May Day festivities, complete with snow on the flightdeck. Any optimism that the 'Valley's' crew might have entertained about the occasion was squashed with the report that the city's pubs would be closed. Upon departure on 4 May the 'Sundowners' participated in an aerial parade over Oslo, flying in a formation that spelt the name of Norway's king, Haakon VII.

Still far from home, *Valley Forge* steamed for California by way of New York and the Panama Canal. The vessel dropped anchor at San Diego on 11 June, 274 days since departure, completing the first world cruise by an American carrier since World War 2. In those nine months the squadron had lost two F8Fs, with another damaged in a landing accident. The 'Sundowners' would see more of *Valley Forge* in years to come.

Shortly after returning Rogers was relieved by Lt Cdr David R Flynn in July 1948. The next month, in another US Navy-wide squadron redesignation scheme, VF-11A became became VF-111, and the 'triple

CAG-11's patch for the 1948 deployment showed the various squadrons embarked, namely VF-11A, 'Fighting 12' (VF-12A), VA-11A and the old Torpedo 11 insignia of VA-12A (*via Tailhook Association*)

CAG-11 commanding officers for the world cruise (from left to right) are Lt Cdr R S Rogers (VF-11A), Cdr R L Fowler (CAG), Cdr M C Hoffman (VF-12A), Lt Cdrs R A Boyd (VA-11A), and G B Riley (VA-12A). Riley was relieved by L B Green in January 1948 (*via Tailhook Association*)

Valley Forge returns to San Diego with CAG-11 after its world cruise. The deployment began as a standard WestPac, but was extended while the task group steamed along the China coast. Eight months after departure the ship returned to San Diego via the Suez Canal, Gibraltar, Norway, New York and the Panama Canal (*via Tailhook Association*)

The squadron upgraded to the 'dash two' Bearcat in March 1949, and six months later VF-111 participated in an at-sea airshow for dignitaries aboard *Valley Forge*. 'V 01' is the commanding officer's aircraft, assigned to Cdr David R Flynn. BuNo 121746 was an F8F-2 with four 20 mm cannon in place of 0.50-cal machine guns in the original model. However, late that year VF-111 began converting to F9F Panther jets (*via Tailhook Association*)

sticks' designation would remain for the rest of the 'Sundowners'' existence. By then the squadron had converted to the F8F-2, losing two pilots in a collision that September.

In the cash-strapped interwar era, flight time was hard to obtain, harder still at sea. The squadron made only three brief at-sea periods in the 13 months between October 1948 and November 1949 totalling just 23 days, mainly embarked for carrier refresher training.

The next step in the 'Sundowners'' saga would take them to the next level of aviation progress.

The four squadrons of CAG-11 pose for a photograph at NAS North Island, San Diego, in August 1949. The 24 men in the front two rows include Cdr Adolf L Siegener, the new CAG, and his staff. The enlisted men are bare-headed because the photographer thought that their hats would result in too much white in the picture! (*Steve Wells*)

THE JET AGE

VF-111 entered the jet age in December 1949 with the arrival of its first Grumman F9F-2 Panthers. It was a signal event, as the squadron retained its Panthers until 1953, when swept-wing Cougars appeared.

Although not the first US Navy jet, the F9F represented a landmark in naval aviation history. McDonnell's FH/FD-1 Phantom had entered service in 1947 but it had seen very limited use as only 61 were built. That same year the North American FJ-1 Fury offered better performance, but just 33 were purchased. Both served mainly as what a later generation would term 'technology demonstrators'. Another McDonnell product was the very capable twin-engined F2H Banshee, which reached the fleet in March 1949, and would remain in service for a decade. Two months later the first Panthers reached VF-51 (which had debuted the Fury), and they remained operational until 1958. The F9F's big advantage over the F2H was in the number built – nearly 1400 Panthers were made versus fewer than 900 Banshees.

With a new aeroplane came a new commanding officer for VF-111 in Lt Cdr William T Amen, who relieved Lt Cdr Flynn in February 1950. Amen had flown FM-2 Wildcats in World War 2, serving as executive officer of Composite Squadron (VC) 82 aboard USS *Anzio* (CVE-57) from October 1944 to March 1945.

Under Tom Amen VF-111 began learning how to operate its new equipment. Panthers offered a significant increase in performance over the Bearcat – nearly 30 percent more top speed (574 to 447 mph), twice the cruise speed and greater ceiling and sustained climb rate. And despite higher landing speeds over piston-engined fighters, pilots readily took to the jet's landing characteristics. One CAG-11 account stated, 'It is generally felt that carrier landings in the F9F-2 type aircraft are accomplished with far greater ease than in conventional types. No major problems have been encountered'.

Because LSOs did not have as much speed indication with jets as with propeller-driven aircraft, CAG-11 considered it 'highly desirable' to have 200 yards 'in the groove' astern of the carrier to allow minor corrections for line-up and speed. The Panther's excellent visibility eased pilot tasking, affording an unimpeded view of the LSO. The pilot was able to make minor corrections in the groove while remaining under LSO control, but some aviators tended to withhold their speed reduction until they were in 'the straightaway', requiring greater loss of excess speed in the groove, sometimes with settling at 'the ramp'.

Catapult launches in the F9F could be tricky in low relative wind at high launch weights, as warm air and the low thrust of the Pratt & Whitney J42-P-6 engine created a marginal safety cushion. Pilots found that later-block 'dash twos' were preferable because they had friction locks on the throttles, whereas earlier variants could allow the accidental reduction of power. Two degrees back (nose up) tab setting was recommended.

A transition patch showing the 1948 redesignation VF-111 while retaining the original Wildcats downing a red sun (*via Tailhook Association*)

Conversion to jets brought a short-lived variation to the traditional 'Sundowners' emblem showing two Wildcats. F9F Panther silhouettes replaced the F4Fs, with the addition of the pseudo-Latin phrase *'Illegitimus non carborundum'* (*via Henk van der Lugt*)

Despite the obvious advantages of jets, there were problems. For instance, the J42 engine's 300-hour operating limit forced more work on maintenance personnel. Additionally, nose wheels fractured in high sink-rate landings that could damage the strut. Nevertheless, the 'Sundowners' were confident of themselves and their equipment when the next war unexpectedly arose.

KOREA

In the early hours of 25 June 1950, North Korean forces smashed across the border in a full-scale assault on South Korea. Thus began a three-year war that diplomats denigrated as a 'conflict'. VF-111 would be intimately involved. In response to the Korean crisis, USS *Philippine Sea* (CV-47), with CVG-11 embarked, deployed from California on 5 July. Leading the air group was an old CAG-11 hand, Cdr Raymond 'Sully' Vogel, who had been Clarence White's 'Sundowner' executive officer on Guadalcanal in 1943. The air group was in combat one month after leaving San Diego, flying reconnaissance and interdiction missions over Korea as part of TF-77.

CAG Vogel led from the front, but he was lost early in the cruise. On 19 August he attacked flak batteries during a strike against bridges near Seoul. His Corsair was badly hit and he died in the bailout. Vogel was succeeded by Cdr Ralph Weymouth, skipper of VF-112, who had flown Douglas SBDs in 1942-44.

The Korean War involved periods of sustained flight operations, sometimes approaching 140 sorties per carrier per day. This routine continued through repeated line periods, and although combat attrition was always a threat, the greater danger lay in routine operations. Indeed, CAG-11 lost seven Panthers from early July through to late September, only two of which fell to enemy action. The more common causes were 'cold cat shots' with insufficient momentum to launch a laden F9F, or fuel exhaustion.

On 18 September the squadron lost a Panther (BuNo 123441) when Ens Earl R Reimers became separated from Amen's division while strafing locomotives. Reimers ran out of fuel and ditched offshore, being recovered by helicopter. A loss six days later put the 'Sundowners' into the record books in an unusual way. Lt C C Dace's jet was hit by AA near Chorwon, just south of the 38th parallel. He coaxed his stricken Panther (BuNo 123445) out over the Yellow Sea, whereupon he ejected and was rescued by the destroyer USS *Chevalier* (DD-805). Dace had almost certainly become the first Naval Aviator to successfully eject in combat.

Far worse losses were incurred during a recovery on 29 September when Ens J Omvig (BuNo 123432) crashed through the barriers, seriously injuring two sailors. Five aircraft sustained major damage and seven lesser harm. Omvig emerged from the wreckage unhurt.

In early November, as United Nations' forces pushed the North Koreans back in the direction of the Chinese border, the strategic situation abruptly shifted. Contrary to Gen Douglas MacArthur's view, Peking suddenly committed large numbers of Chinese troops to Korea. Almost overnight the complexion of the Korean War changed again. The situation turned on logistics. Thus, MacArthur sought approval to

The CAG-11 patch for the Korean War emphasised the United Nations' mission, with the group's squadrons surrounding the organisation's distinctive emblem – VF-111 and VF-112 'Fighting Twelve' (F9F-2s) on the top row, VA-113 'Stingers' and VA-114 'Executioners' (F4U-4s) in the middle and VA-115 'Arabs' (AD-4s) at the bottom. Not represented on the patch were detachments from VC-3 (nightfighters), VC-61 (photo-reconnaissance, VC-11 (electronic warfare) and HU-1 (helicopter search and rescue) (*via Tailhook Association*)

destroy the Yalu River bridges sustaining the communist drive out of Manchuria. After some waffling, the American joint chiefs approved such an offensive, with serious qualifications.

TF-77 had been fully engaged in interdiction and close air support. Now it was tasked to join the strategic air campaign, with the inherent precision of carrier aircraft over high-level bombers. But geopolitical fears in Washington, D.C. required the aviators only to bomb the southern half of the bridges, leaving communist AA guns inviolate on the north bank. It was that kind of war.

Aside from heavy and light calibre AA guns, the defenders had something new – Soviet MiG-15 jet fighters. The swept-winged MiGs were first encountered on 8 November during a USAF attack on the Sinuiju bridges near the mouth of the Yalu. 16th Fighter Squadron F-80C pilot Lt Russell Brown was credited with the first jet-versus-jet victory in history, although decades would pass before it was learned that his Russian opponent had in fact returned to base.

The next morning it was the 'tailhookers'' turn. Thus far the US Navy had made three aerial kills over Korea – two Yak-9 fighters destroyed by *Valley Forge* Panthers in July and an Il-4 transport by one of its Corsairs in September.

The 139th Guards Fighter Air Regiment (GvIAP), based at the Antung complex, was responsible for protecting the Sinuiju bridges. The scramble that morning was led by the regimental commander,

Maj Bochkov, while Capt Mikhail Grachev led the 1st Squadron into its initial combat. Launching in singles, pairs and treys, the MiGs arrived piecemeal.

Flying Target CAP was Tom Amen (in a VF-112 jet) with his 'Sundowner' division. The Russians correctly identified the Panthers and Corsairs, but described the Skyraiders as F6F Hellcats. Apparently none of the carrier pilots saw all seven MiGs, as only four were reported. Consequently, the combat became a strung-out, sprawling dogfight, in and out of the clouds. When the first two MiGs pounced, the Corsairs and Skyraiders broke into the threat, forcing an overshoot. Meanwhile, Amen checked his tail, noted an unidentified aircraft closing, and turned his division to meet the bogey. In a climbing chase from 4000 ft to 15,000 ft, Amen pursued, remaining in the MiG's blind spot. The enemy pilot yawed his fighter, apparently trying to find

Lt Cdr William T Amen led the 'Sundowners' on their first Korean War deployment. On 9 November 1950 he made aviation history by scoring the first air-to-air victory in jet combat when he downed a Soviet MiG-15. He completed the *Philippine Sea* cruise and was later made commander the air group (*via Henk van der Lugt*)

the F9Fs, but allowed Amen and his wingman George Holloman to close the distance. Both 'Sundowners' fired and one or both scored hits.

The Russian nosed into a near-vertical dive that Amen could not easily follow. His F9F entered buffet while approaching terminal velocity, forcing him to fight rudder reversal. Nevertheless, he fired as the MiG crossed his sight, and apparently put more 20 mm rounds into the target. At about 3000 ft Amen was astonished to see his quarry roll inverted and start to pull through. The skipper thought, 'Either he's nuts or he's got a wonderful aeroplane'. As Amen loaded heavy G onto himself to recover from his dive at merely 200 ft, he lost sight of his victim. However, Holloman saw the MiG crater a hillside, erupting in a fireball that ignited surrounding trees. Thus died Mikhail Grachev, the first pilot killed in jet-versus-jet combat.

The Russians believed they had downed five or six Americans, including two or three that AA gunners attributed to Grachev. Maj Bochkov claimed a 'Hellcat', but a subsequent debrief rightly concluded that 'the 139th GvIAP flew alone and unorganised'.

Amen's kill was credited as the 36th Allied aerial victory of the war. However, more were close at hand. Later that day *Valley Forge* F9Fs downed two more MiGs, while the Russians in turn shot up an RB-29 that crashed on return to Japan. In its subsequent cruise report, CAG-11 stated;

'The basic conception of combat in jet fighters has previously been that due to tremendous speeds the firing time allowed would restrict tactics to a single pass and breakaway for each aeroplane in a division, and then a complete repositioning for a second attack. It was also thought that the evasive manoeuvres of the attacked fighter would prevent anything other than the single attack. Combat with the MiG-15 has proven otherwise, although it should be noted that without a single exception pilots rated the enemy pilots as poor, and it must be assumed that they did not fight their jet to its best advantage.

'In the engagement with the MiG-15, no difficulty was experienced in gaining an advantageous tail position, and holding this position for sufficient time to press an attack. The only evasive manoeuvre that could not be countered was the diving escape, but before this could be executed, ample attack time had been allowed. If the enemy jet could only resort to diving to escape, a successful encounter must be acknowledged, as friendly aircraft were safe from attack during this manoeuvre.

'The proven "scissors" tactics, as employed by conventional aircraft, were used to good advantage in gaining the offensive. The enemy jets that would stay in an encounter for any length of time were quickly confused and put on the defensive.

'Altitude advantages of more than a few thousand feet were found to be unsatisfactory because of the spotting problems. Unless below, or a little above, sight contact could not be gained or maintained. However, this was not considered to be serious, as a jet fighter can stay at maximum speed in a level attitude, and the element of surprise is as great when closing from below, or level, when commenced from the greater distances involved in jet-versus-jet combat as it would be if a diving attack from altitude were made.

The 'Sundowners'' second Korean War cruise was aboard *Valley Forge* with ATG-1 from October 1951 to July 1952 (*via Tailhook Association*)

'The employment of two-aeroplane sections was found to be completely satisfactory against the relatively uncoordinated enemy jets. However, the four-aeroplane division should be used in cases of teamwork or coordinated attacks by the enemy.'

Throughout the rest of November CAG-11 recorded five MiG encounters without success. Inoperative guns cost some pilots victories, including CAG Weymouth. The cause was traced to inadequate T-2 gun heaters, which often failed because of broken wiring. All heaters were removed and/or replaced, guns cleaned and examined, worn parts replaced and excess lubrication removed.

In assessing the early jet-versus-jet combats, *Philippine Sea's* staff concluded;

'Jets are comfortable, quiet, dependable and handle well in the air. They have shown themselves capable of sustaining considerable damage and still be fit to return to the carrier. There is no undue concern toward making water landings. But fewer flying hours equals less opportunity to engage the enemy than prop pilots.

'Employment of jets by the enemy proved to be a morale booster, as reflected in the attitude of the rest of the air group toward the Panther units, and in the realisation by our fighter pilots that their efforts were not going unrecognised.'

An assessment of the F9F-2 versus the MiG-15 was contained in the *Naval Aviation Confidential Bulletin* for August 1951. It made several salient points;

'First, be on the offensive. The MiG-15 must be spotted first and broken into at once. Speeds are too high to wait even 30 seconds.

'Second, all hands must have swivel heads, even while trying to stay with the leader during flight.

'Third, never try to get away from a MiG in a dive.

'Fourth, at moderate speeds use a tight turn to get a MiG off your tail.

'Fifth, attempt to fire in front of the MiG when out of effective range to induce him to manoeuvre, thereby closing on him in the turns that follow.'

One pilot stated bluntly, 'The MiG-15 completely outclasses the F9F. The Panther possibly could outturn the MiG, but that's purely defensive, and you can't fight a war that way'.

Some Panther pilots expressed a desire for North American FJ-2s, feeling that swept-wing fighters were necessary to meet the MiG-15 on more equal terms. However, no Furies were ever deployed to Korea during the war.

Near the end of the cruise in March 1951, the air group commented upon the declining opportunities for F9F pilots to fly sufficient hours. Because jet pilots only averaged 4.9 hours per month, CVG-11 recommended reducing the pilot ratio from 1.3 to 1.1 and embarking fewer jets.

During the 1950-51 *Philippine Sea* combat cruise VF-111 lost six aircraft, only one to enemy action. After seven months on cruise, CAG-11 'crossdecked' with CAG-2 from *Valley Forge* and rode 'Happy Valley' to San Diego in early April 1951.

VALLEY FORGE 1951-52

In November 1951 the 'Sundowners' were reunited with *Valley Forge*, three-and-a-half years after their historic world cruise. The vessel left San Diego embarking Air Task Group One (ATG-1) under Cdr C H Crabill Jr.

Air task groups were an expedient forced upon naval aviation by interwar budget cuts. Unable to sustain a full establishment of air groups with permanently assigned squadrons, the flying admirals played 'mix and match' by periodically assigning units to an ATG. The advantage was that, as in Korea, air groups could be customised to suit the most likely operational requirements. Thus, as the war progressed and the need for jet fighters diminished, more emphasis could be placed on attack aircraft – primarily F4U Corsairs and AD Skyraiders. However, due to its impromptu nature, ATG-1's squadrons were

Cdr Frank Welch (left) relieves Lt Cdr W T Amen as CO on 6 June 1951. Welch was killed in a carrier landing on 29 October that same year (*via Henk van der Lugt*)

Pilots of ATG-1 prepare to man aircraft during *Valley Forge's* 1951-52 deployment. 'Flying Circus' pilots of VF-653 (a Reserve F4U-4 Corsair squadron) are wearing the polka dot helmets (*via Tailhook Association*)

unable to train or fully operate together before departure. The group's success was testament to the overall quality of aircrews and leaders.

For their second Korean War cruise the 'Sundowners' were led by Cdr Frank Welch Jr, a 1941 Annapolis graduate. He deployed with 25 pilots for 16 Panthers, which gave the unit a pilot-to-seat ratio of 1.5 to one. This was ample because it provided some 'velvet' for attrition and illness. Four F9F photo-reconnaissance pilots also flew with VF-111 on occasion too. As experience later demonstrated, a ratio of less than 1.2-to-1 forced extra responsibility upon the remaining pilots, who sometimes had to launch two or three times on flying days.

Tragedy struck on 29 October when Cdr Welch's Panther (BuNo 127177) crashed into the sea from the landing pattern. He was succeeded by Lt Cdr John W Ramsey, who held excellent 'Sundowner' credentials, having flown with VF-11 at Guadalcanal in 1943.

ATG-1 aircrews attended an 'in-chop' briefing aboard USS *Bon Homme Richard* (CV-31), whose CAG-101 pilots were completing their deployment. Thus, the newcomers benefited from the knowledge of the old hands who had learned the best way to operate in Korean airspace. *Valley Forge* began its first line period in December, with jets taking damage on 16 occasions versus 35 for propeller-driven aircraft. The jet squadrons escaped personnel casualties on the first line period, but ATG-1 lost two Corsair pilots in a collision, one possibly to structural failure, with another F4U pilot missing after ditching. Additionally, a Skyraider crew was captured and a single-seat AD pilot drowned.

On 3 January 1952 'Sundowner' Earl Reimers' Panther (BuNo 127132) sustained flak damage, causing a fuel leak that forced a ditching in Songjin Harbour. Reimers received minor injuries, but was recovered by a minesweeper. A CAG-11 veteran, he had put a *Philippine Sea* F9F in the water during the 1950 cruise, too.

During the second line period (30 January to 22 February) the air group lost four Corsairs, three Skyraiders and two Panthers. On 19 February, Lt W P Johnson of VF-111 ditched near the ship following a flameout, being rescued by the *Valley Forge* helicopter. The ship's action report contains internal contradictions, variously listing both Johnson and VF-52's Lt(jg) D F Tatum in that event. Later the document specifies that Tatum was the Panther pilot killed that day.

Most overland missions involved rail cuts, which the communists not only sought to prevent but worked industriously to repair. Consequently, the process was continuous for both sides. In February ATG-1 staff noted a trend in enemy AAA, with increasing reliance upon mobile 37 mm weapons. Curiously, the huge majority of battle damage was inflicted on Panthers rather than the slower Skyraiders and Corsairs.

Meanwhile, the 'Sundowners' coped with human and materiel shortages. In April it was noted, 'Once the pilot per seat ratio drops below 1.5 for props and 1.2 for jets, the law of diminishing returns becomes evident, as some of the pilots become grounded for various medical reasons, requiring the remainder to fly more, thereby heightening in turn their fatigue level'. But even when replacement pilots were requested immediately after each loss, inevitable delays occurred due to the need for inoculations, etc. ATG-1 suggested a permanent replacement pool under Commander Fleet Air Japan, where carrier qualifications could be maintained. Attrition continued through the next two line periods, with three pilots and eight aircraft being lost from 14 April to 16 May. Two Panthers were destroyed on 2 May when they crashed due to fuel starvation after being diverted to Koryo. Lt(jg)s W S Parr and R J Lear were retrieved – evidently VF-52 pilots possibly flying VF-111 jets.

During May and June aircrews noted 45 damaged locomotives in a rail 'graveyard' at Chongjin, plus some 15 more at the Wonsan marshalling and repair yard. However, that visible testament to the aviators' effectiveness was matched by increasingly capable AAA, and mission planners required more recent tactical information. Flak suppressors especially needed current intelligence ('hot dope') for maximum effectiveness for their ordnance – mainly variable-timed fused and impact bombs, plus napalm and 20 mm ammunition.

Throughout the deployment ATG-1 logged 7113 sorties – 3667 by jets, 1525 by F4Us and 1921 by Skyraiders. Thus, jet fighters typically flew 47 percent of all sorties and reconnaissance F9Fs another four percent. The ship's end of cruise report concluded that the ATG concept was 'considered sound in that it provides carrier aviation with an important additional flexibility which must be available if naval aviation is to continue to progress'.

'Happy Valley' returned to the West Coast in July 1952, at which point the Korean War still had 12 months to run. Cdr Arthur E Vickery assumed command of VF-111 in September, and the next month the unit received the latest Panther variant when F9F-5s arrived. The 'Sundowners' quickly adapted to their new mounts, sending gunnery detachments to NAAS El Centro, California, in October.

The new Panther was generally considered to be an improvement on the F9F-2 (only 109 interim F9F-4s were built). Visibly different to the earlier variant thanks to its higher vertical stabiliser, the 'dash five' was rated about 25 knots faster, although it possessed a lower service ceiling (42,800 ft compared to 44,600 ft). Range and rate of climb were comparable.

Jet pilots with World War 2 experience often drew unfavourable comparisons between the effectiveness of piston-engined aircraft in the previous conflict and what was seen in Korea. Whereas an SBD Dauntless making a 70-degree dive at 240 knots was seldom hit in 1942-45, Panthers attacking at twice that speed in a 30-degree dive frequently sustained battle damage. Comparisons for a 2000-ft recovery meant that Dauntlesses could drop at 2400 ft and Panthers at 3200 ft. Furthermore, 'own ordnance' blast damage forced most jet squadrons to adopt a minimum altitude of 3000 ft over the target, which in turn reduced accuracy.

The solution suggested by combat-experienced fighter-bomber pilots was the 'point blank' attack – a 35 to 40 degree dive angle beginning at 75 percent power and a speed of 230 knots, with the speed brake extended. The recommended release height was 1800 ft over the target, then retracting the brake and beginning a five-G pullout. Egressing at 100 percent power, the use of delayed-action bombs could eliminate blast damage to trailing aircraft. The 'point blank' technique produced

V 115 (BuNo 127173) on the deck of *Valley Forge* during its 1951-52 Korean War deployment. The Panther sports some 40 mission markers, each sortie denoted by a white bomb (*via Tailhook Association*)

results against lightly defended targets, but it still put jets well within range of small-calibre weapons.

VF-111 remained at Miramar until March 1953 when it again deployed with ATG-1.

BOXER-LAKE CHAMPLAIN 1953

For their third Korean War deployment the 'Sundowners' boarded a carrier new to VF-111, USS *Boxer*, now designated CVA-21. In October 1952 the Navy had decided to distinguish aircraft carriers by their primary roles. Therefore, ships designated CV became either attack carriers (CVA) or antisubmarine carriers (CVS). Escort (CVE) and light (CVL) carriers retained their previous designators.

Again assigned to ATG-1, VF-111 was one of three fighter squadrons aboard *Boxer*. Although aerial combat was extremely rare (carrier-based aviators shot down just 12 aircraft during the war), Cdr L A Whitney's group also embarked VF-52 and VF-151.

Boxer deployed for WestPac in late March 1953, leaving Yokosuka, Japan, on 10 May for the first line period. Thus began the ship's fourth combat deployment, prompting TF-77 commander Rear Adm Apollo Soucek to signal, 'Glad to have the tough old veteran back with us'. *Boxer* had been deployed 19 of the 25 months between August 1950 and September 1952.

The May and June priorities were interdiction of northeastern Korean transport, strikes on storage areas and electric power systems and close air support. Additionally, TF-77 air groups cooperated with the USAF's Fifth Air Force in keeping the pressure on communist forces south of the Yalu River.

After ATG-1 launched 63 sorties on its first day back, Soucek, riding USS *Princeton* (CV-37), added, 'Performance *Boxer* and her air group today very fine. My forecast – soon you will be better than any previous *Boxer* air group, and that's pretty good'. The next day the ship logged 109 combat sorties.

Commander Seventh Fleet, Vice Adm J J 'Jocko' Clark, also sent a message in appreciation of *Boxer's* 'important contribution to the Korean conflict by remaining in the operating area at a critical period of the campaign for a period of 38 days and delivering over 2600 air

ATG-1 Panthers are parked aft aboard *Boxer* in 1953. Besides VF-111, other F9Fs belonged to VF-52 (S 200 modexes) and VF-151 (H 300). However, the Sundowners' F9F-5s had difficulty operating with *Boxer's* old-model catapults so the squadron 'cross-decked' to *Lake Champlain* to complete the deployment (*Archibald McCleish via Henk van der Lugt*)

sorties against the enemy'. In that time the air group lost eight aeroplanes and one pilot to all causes, including a 'Sundowner' jet. On 19 June, returning from a photo escort, Lt D H Opsahl ran short of fuel and ditched BuNo 126204 at sea. Although rescued by helicopter, he had sustained back injuries that removed him from flight status until he could be fully evaluated.

Various problems were encountered operating F9F-5s that led to VF-111 leaving *Boxer*. On occasion the carrier was unable to launch aircraft due to both insufficient wind over the deck and the unsuitability of its catapults, and aeroplane handlers had difficulty

Plane handlers pushing V106 on board *Boxer* in 1953. A plane captain sits in the cockpit to 'ride the brakes', preventing the seven-ton Panther from rolling into another aircraft (*Archibald McCleish via Henk van der Lugt*)

manoeuvring the larger Panther on the number two elevator. Additionally, the incompatibility of a 'dash two' and 'dash five' flying mixed sections prompted a decision to cross-deck VF-111 to another ship upon the carrier's return to Japan.

Following the first line period on 21 June, *Boxer* steamed to Sasebo, where Cdr Vickery was directed to move VF-111 to USS *Lake Champlain* (CVA-39), which embarked CAG-4 under Cdr J R Sweeney. 'The Champ' had left the East Coast in April, thus becoming only the second Atlantic Fleet carrier to deploy to Korea after USS *Leyte* (CVA-32) in 1950. On 30 June the 'Sundowners' F9F-5s were exchanged for *Lake Champlain's* VF-44 F4U-4 Corsairs owing to the limitations of *Boxer's* H4B catapult, which had difficulty launching combat-loaded Panthers. Conversely, 'The Champ' had more efficient H8 catapults, and also carried a greater quantity of jet fuel.

Lake Champlain departed Sasebo on 11 July, embarking Vickery's 15 F9F-5s partnered with the F2H Banshees of VF-22 and VF-62. After ATG-1, this was only the second time that three jet squadrons had been embarked in one carrier during the war. In its cruise report, *Lake Champlain* described the 'Sundowners' as 'a seasoned, experienced unit, having completed, prior to reporting, 46 days of "on the line" operations'. However, CAG-4 conceded that 15 days without flying was 'excessive' for a jet squadron. Furthermore, in its time ashore VF-111 had some deferred maintenance that was not easily rectified aboard the new carrier. The ship's unfamiliarity with the F9F-5 also led to problems during the 'Sundowners' time aboard. Aircraft handlers unwittingly damaged Panthers on ten occasions, aggravating the lack of sufficient spare parts. The most-damaged parts were control surfaces and wing flaps, although constant maintenance kept most of the Panthers in 'up' status.

Subsequently, CAG-4 reported, 'The F9F is short-legged when compared to the F2H. During this period of comparative operations it was learned that 800 lbs is not a low state, and that it is acceptable to wave off an F9F in its approach with 450 lbs if the aeroplane following has only 250 lbs. Generally, for the F9F it was found that the margin of time is very slim when working a 90-minute schedule. The F2H proved to have a much more comfortable margin'. But the Banshee was limited to carrying just 1400 lbs of ordnance, while the F9F could carry 2000 lbs off the H8 catapult.

During the first two days 'on the line' CAG-4 worked without updated tactical data such as the location of the 'bomb line' and enemy defences. An oversight while in-port at Yokosuka had prevented that important information from being distributed, but the dedicated intelligence officers thereafter made up the deficit. In fact, Vickery's pilots were impressed with the professionalism of *Lake Champlain's* assistant intelligence officers. With some experience, VF-111 aviators developed a preference for 'the Champ's' type of flight chart when it came to displaying navigation and tactical data.

The carrier's cruise report took special note of survival equipment, stating, 'Pilots for the main part were dissatisfied with the present combat flight uniform which consists of G-suit, coverall, survival vest and Mae West. It is felt that a one-piece survival suit is desirable. The average time to "suit up" is now about seven minutes'.

With three years of combat experience, the US Navy recognised that aircrew survival had become a specialised field. CAG-4 called for streamlining survival training and the development of better survival radios than the AN/PRC-17s installed in pararafts. 'All pilots want a survival radio' the air group stated, 'but the AN/PRC-17 is definitely not the answer'.

Panthers and Banshees concentrated on 'Cherokee' strikes in what later generations would know as route packages or kill boxes. The most frequent targets were bridges in the unending battle against communist transport and logistics, as TF-77 launched record numbers of sorties on 23-25 July. Then, amid rumors of an impending ceasefire, on 26 and 27 July *Lake Champlain* sent strikers against airfields in North Korea so as to keep them unusable.

On the morning of 27 July the task force received notice of the ceasefire, with the armistice to take effect at 2200 hrs. Meanwhile, the 'Sundowners'' last Korean War action involved Lt(jg) Arthur R Loomer, Ens James J McGinnnis, Lt James M Riggan, and Lt(jg) William A Finlay Jr. The division was vectored to Yonpo airfield, southwest of Hungnam. It was also the last combat flight to launch from *Lake Champlain*. CTF-77 wanted the airfield kept neutralised, though as part of the impending settlement the communists had pledged not to operate MiGs from Yonpo.

Briefed to crater the runway, Loomer's flight encountered no opposition as it approached the target. The 'Sundowners' released their bombs at 1730 hrs, and the last to attack was Bill Finlay in BuNo 126037. He was credited with dropping the US Navy's last bombs of the war. The division returned to the ship after 1.6 hours aloft.

In their brief period of combat from 'The Champ', 'Sundowner' pilots expended 1930 bombs totalling 211 tons, plus 72 rockets and some 32,000 rounds of 20 mm. In turn, VF-111 sustained three battle-damaged F9Fs (plus one Panther taxied into another aircraft), compared to three Banshees damaged and one missing. The F2H pilots were especially aggressive in low-level attacks, returning with bomb blast damage on six or seven occasions.

Ordnance officers recommended that the F9F-5's two inboard Mk 51 bomb racks be removed and, to compensate, load 500-lb bombs on the inboard Mk 14 launchers. That configuration was expected to reduce fuel consumption, increase cruise speed and ceiling and provide 90-minute cycle times without 'low fuel state' on return to the ship.

Two days after the ceasefire the air group was flying again, providing Rescue CAP flights and conducting gunnery training. Over the next two months the ship cycled in and out of port at Yokosuka and Sasebo. The 'Sundowners'' only notable incident occurred with a hard landing on 17 October. During that period (10 October to 11 November) the pilots logged 326 hours for an average of 14 hours apiece in nine flights.

Relieved on station by *Kearsarge* in mid-October, *Lake Champlain* transferred VF-111 to *Boxer*, which returned to San Diego in late November.

In three Korean War deployments VF-111 apparently lost no permanently assigned pilots – Lt(jg) Alan Hoff of VC-61, killed in March 1952, occasionally flew with VF-111. At least ten Panthers were

Sailors crowd around V134 aboard *Lake Champlain* in 1953. The assigned pilot was Lt(jg) Rollo Young, but on 27 July BuNo 126037 was flown by Lt(jg) W A Finlay, who dropped the squadron's last bombs of the Korean War. The Panther's nose cone has been pulled forward to permit access to the four 20 mm cannon (*Archibald McCleish via Henk van der Lugt*)

An errant VF-111 F9F-5 (BuNo 126037, as seen above) returns to *Lake Champlain* during post-armistice operations in 1953. After erroneously landing aboard USS *Yorktown* (CVA-10), the 'Sundowners' jet received graffiti applied by its 'hosts.' Among the verbage is 'Landed by the Fighting Lady', and the modex 134 has been altered to 184. All ATG-1 squadrons retained their original tail codes, hence the *Valley Forge* V symbol has been modified to a *Yorktown* M. This was the same aircraft that dropped the squadron's last bombs of the war whilst being flown by Lt(jg) William A Finlay Jr (*Henk van der Lugt*)

lost to all causes while deployed, although only three were attributed to enemy action.

SWEPT WINGS

The 'Sundowners' had barely returned to Miramar when they began the significant task of transitioning to a swept-wing aircraft. The F9F-6 and subsequent models were named Cougars to distinguish them from the straight-wing Panthers, and VF-111 received its first 'dash six' models in December 1953.

Other squadrons had accepted F9F-6s a year earlier, so the Cougar's reputation was well established. Top speed was boosted to 647 mph, some 40 mph better than the F9F-5, but otherwise pilots found little difference in flight characteristics. Of particular importance to tailhook

VF-111 converted from F9F-5 Panthers to swept-wing F9F-6s at the end of 1953 and took them to sea in USS *Wasp* (CVA-18) the next year. This Cougar sits on the deck-edge elevator as the pilot receives taxi instructions from the plane director (*via Henk van der Lugt*)

The 'Sundowners'' 1954 squadron board with Cdr A J Knudson and his 27 officers, including pilots and department heads. The unit made no deployments in 1954 or 1955 (*via Tailhook Association*)

aviators was the fact that the new fighter required only about three knots more airspeed in the carrier pattern. However, the 'Sundowners' never deployed with the new fighter in the 18 months they flew the 'dash six' to June 1955. Leading the unit during most of the F9F-6 era was Cdr A J 'Gus' Knudson, who assumed command in 1954.

Of more significance to VF-111 was the F9F-8, with similar performance to the previous Cougar. However, the fighter's in-flight refuelling probe represented an important growth in carrier fighter capability. Its Pratt & Whitney J48 was rated at 7250 lbs thrust, which was 200 lbs more than the same powerplant in the F9F-5. Additionally, from mid-1956 onward, Cougars were armed with AIM-9 Sidewinder missiles. The 'Sundowners'' only F9F-8 deployment came that year aboard USS *Lexington* (CVA-16), again as part of ATG-1 teamed with VF-52's F2H-3 Banshees and VF-151's F7U-3 Cutlasses. 'Lady Lex' departed in May 1956, joining the Seventh Fleet at Yokosuka. The air group conducted exercises and search and rescue missions off the China coast, and the ship returned to San Diego just in time for Christmas.

VF-111's next fighter was another swept-wing transonic design, North American's FJ-3 Fury, which closely resembled the F-86. First

F9F-8 U113 (BuNo 141196) rides the catapult aboard *Lexington* in 1956 – 'the Sundowners'' only cruise with the late-model Cougar. By that date the US Navy had largely switched from the previous overall gloss blue to a two-tone scheme of matt gull grey over white (*via Tailhook Association*)

VF-111 won the day-fighter aerial gunnery championship in April 1958 under Cdr F E Miller, with Lt P H Speer and Lts(jg) H L Landry, R Mudgett and D Macintyre. Note the numeral '1' in the air group's star emblem, signifying the 'Sundowners'' ranking (*Dick Mudgett via Tailhook*)

Bennington steams with ATG-4 embarked for the 1958-59 cruise to the Western Pacific. VF-111 flew FJ-3 Furies at the time, prepared to engage communist Chinese aircraft during the continuing Formosa Strait crisis (*via Tailhook Association*)

flown in December 1953, the Fury was rated at 680 mph, with a combat-loaded ceiling of nearly 50,000 ft. Its 8000-ft per minute rate of climb endeared it to task force commanders as an interceptor far better than the F9F-8's 5700-ft per minute.

The squadron transitioned to the Fury in 1957 and, in April 1958, competed in the annual gunnery meet at NAS El Centro. Cdr F E Miller led the 'Sundowners' to victory in the day fighter category shortly before turning over to Cdr R W Huxford. One of the team's Fury pilots was Lt Paul Speer, who would claim a MiG kill while leading VF-211 some nine years later .

Subsequently, VF-111 deployed in USS *Bennington* (CVA-20) with ATG-4 from August 1958 to January 1959. This proved to be the last of ATG-4's three cruises.

The Western Pacific experienced unusual turmoil that year. In the Peoples' Republic of China (PRC), Mao Tse-Tung's 'Great Leap Forward' had begun, but Peking looked outward as well. China's increasingly hostile actions prompted deployment of additional carriers to WestPac beyond the two already there. On 21 August *Bennington* cut short its work-ups and steamed westward. Two days later PRC artillery opened a heavy, sustained bombardment on the Nationalist-occupied Quemoy Islands. The fighting involved prolonged aerial combat over the Formosa Strait, lasting until October as Nationalist Chinese F-86s clashed with PRC MiG-17s. The Nationalists claimed 31 kills, four with AIM-9Bs, while the communists proclaimed at least 14 victories, although few of the latter were confirmed in the west.

En route to the operating area, ATG-4 aircrews received updated

intelligence briefings. VF-111 learned that the Chinese possessed somewhere between 1800 and 2500 aircraft, including 400+ assigned to its navy. The PRC was known to operate MiG-15s and MiG-17s, plus Il-28 'Beagle' bombers. There were reports of MiG-19s at the time too, but the PRC apparently did not receive 'Farmers' until 1963.

Bennington steamed off the China coast for 43 consecutive days, launching patrols and surveillance aircraft both day and night. The sudden appearance of six attack carriers led the PRC to conclude that America would honour its treaty with Taiwan, and the crisis abated over the next two months. Upon returning to San Diego in January 1959 VF-111 bade farewell to *Bennington*, which was to be refitted as an antisubmarine carrier.

On 19 January 1959 the 'Sundowners'' unbroken lineage from 1942 came to an unexpected end. VF-111 stood down but the next day re-emerged when VA-156 adopted the designation. What prompted such an unusual event has never been explained, although some 'Sundowners' believed that the Japanese government had objected to the squadron's emblem. Supposition held that politicians and bureaucrats in Washington, D.C. ordered the disestablishment, even while knowing that the squadron would be reconstituted. In any case, nothing further was heard of the matter.

VA-156 had existed since 1956, having received the first production F11F-1 Tiger fighters at NAS Moffett Field in March 1957 – never mind that it was designated an attack squadron! The 'Iron Tigers' participated in CAG-11's WestPac deployment aboard USS *Shangri-La* (CVA-38) in 1958. Redesignated VF-111, and still

A 'Sundowner' division over Oahu in September 1958. Three aircraft bear ATG-4's 'shooting star' emblem on the fuselage, while NA 112 has yet to receive it. The squadron deployed in *Bennington* in 1958-59 – the only cruise VF-111 made with the North American fighter (*Henk van der Lugt*)

An overhead view of two VF-111 Furies escorting an F9F-8P photo-reconnaissance Cougar of VFP-61 Detachment K. This photograph was probably taken during the 1958 *Bennington* deployment (*via Tailhook Association*)

'Sundowners'' Tigers in 'finger four'
led by NH101. The latter was the
skipper's aircraft, usually flown
by Cdr R W Huxford, who led the
squadron in 1958-59 (*via Tailhook
Association*)

Tigers prowl Mount Fuji. VF-111
made two WestPac deployments
with F11Fs – *Shangri-La* in 1959
and *Hancock* in 1960-61. This
view was probably taken during
the latter cruise, with a division
stacked downward in right echelon
(*via Tailhook Association*)

flying F11Fs, the squadron
returned to 'Shang' for a cruise
from March to October 1959. It
was the first time the 'Sundowners'
had deployed with their parent air
group since 1951.

George M 'Skip' Furlong was
one of only two pilots who served
in both VA-156 and VF-111. A
former 'white hat', he qualified for
the Naval Academy and graduated
in 1956, receiving his wings the
next year. He recalled;

'VA-156 was a Moffett Field
F11F-1 squadron that deployed to
WestPac in 1957. The VA designation was a misnomer that was never
explained to me. I was sent out as a replacement pilot from Miramar
(VF-121) along with another nugget named "Cheeks" Weeks. VA-156
had had a number of Alpha accidents by the time we arrived, killing
some of its quota of pilots. Upon our return to ConUS, we moved from
Moffett to Miramar and were redesignated VF-111 in CAG-11. I stayed
with the squadron through two more deployments, and flew the
squadron's last F11F to Litchfield Park in 1961 when we transitioned to
F8U-2Ns. Those were wild days. I don't know how any of us ever
survived either in the air or on the ground, but it sure was fun.'

Furlong remained in the US Navy, retiring as a rear admiral in 1986.

The squadron had two skippers during 1959 – Cdrs Jack E Godfrey
and Wayne R Cheal. The latter was a combat-experienced fighter pilot
who had flown Hellcats in VF-81, scoring two victories in 1945.

Following the *Shangri-La* cruise, VF-111 recycled its Tigers for the
next WestPac made by USS *Hancock* (CVA-19), which ran from July
1960 to March 1961 partly in response to increasing tension in Laos –

the 'back door' by which America became fully engaged in Vietnam. In that period Cdr Richard Cyr (a World War 2 'Sundowner') became CAG-11.

While the squadron had never previously flown from 'Hannah', the 'Sundowners' were back among old friends with CAG-11, although

NH 113 on *Shangri-La's* port catapult during WestPac operations in 1959. The squadron took 13 Grumman F11Fs on the cruise, which lasted from March to October (*via Tailhook Assn*)

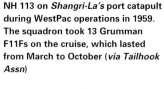

Above left
NH 108 was F8U-2N BuNo 147056 off *Kitty Hawk* in 1963. Redesignated an F-8D, it was converted to F-8P status and sent to the Philippine (*via Tailhook Association*)

Above
To mark the squadron's transition to the supersonic F8U Crusader, in early 1961 VF-111 adopted a mascot in the form of 'Omar', suggested by the enlisted men. It remained a regular feature of unit lore for the next 34 years (*via Tailhook Asociation*)

Left
The 'Sundowners' conducted their initial Crusader carrier qualifications aboard *Kitty Hawk* in 1961. BuNo 148639 was lost while assigned to developmental squadron VX-4 in 1970 (*via Tailhook Association*)

VF-112 had by then become an attack squadron flying A4D-2 Skyhawks. Upon returning to San Francisco *Hancock* began a year-long overhaul, requiring the air group to seek a new home.

FASTER THAN SOUND

In May 1961 VF-111 received the Vought F8U-2N Crusader. It was a milestone not only in the 'Sundowners'' history, but in the progress of naval aviation. As the first genuinely supersonic naval aircraft, the Crusader joined a select circle of tailhook fighters that could outperform most land-based opponents. Previously that honour had gone to the A6M Zero-sen, F4U Corsair and F6F Hellcat. Moreover, the Crusader's high thrust-to-weight ratio enabled it to fight with its nose above the horizon. Under Cdr Homer A Winter, the squadron began exploring the sensational Vought's potential.

Transition to a Mach 1 fighter called for a squadron mascot, and 'Sundowner' enlisted men conceived a triangular stick figure dubbed 'Omar'. Soon, red renderings of 'Omar' appeared throughout squadron spaces, on VF-111 aircraft and in other squadron areas – occasionally on other squadron aircraft too. 'Omar' bespoke of excellent morale, and remained a 'Sundowner' symbol for three decades.

In addition to flying the hottest aircraft in the fleet – the F-4B Phantom II was still three years away – the 'Sundowners' found themselves comfortably aboard USS *Kitty Hawk* (CVA-63), the newest carrier afloat. They flew to the East Coast, boarded the new 'flattop'

'Sundowner' officers pose in this 1963 photograph before the mount of USAF exchange pilot Capt G L Schulstab. Under skipper Charles E Ray, VF-111 adopted the sharksmouth emblem that would remain a squadron trademark through the Phantom II and Tomcat eras (*via Tailhook Association*)

and rode it to California with other CAG-11 squadrons for its two-and-a-half-month shakedown cruise, beginning in September. The east-to-west excursion permitted exercises in the Atlantic and Caribbean, before rounding Cape Horn en route to San Diego. Since the tri-service aircraft designation system took effect on 18 September, 'Sundowners' historian Henk van der Lugt noted that a pilot who launched in an F8U-2N landed in an F-8D! Thus began more than a decade in 'The Last of the Gunfighters'.

When *Kitty Hawk* deployed from October 1963 to July 1964, it was the last time that CAG-11 operated as a fully integrated unit, including VA-112 and VA-113 with A-4Cs, VA-115 with A-1Hs and VF-114's Phantom IIs. In December 1963 carrier air groups became carrier air wings (CVWs), although the CAG (Commander Air Group) terminology remained for Cdrs W H O'Neil and N J Gambrill.

However, it was not certain that VF-111 would make the *Kitty Hawk* cruise. That September CAG-2 was working up for a USS *Midway* (CVA-41) deployment when one of its fighter squadrons, VF-24, was transferred to another wing. Consequently, VF-111 was redesignated VF-26 as the sixth squadron in CVW-2. The change was short-lived (roughly lasting just the first half of September), but reportedly some 'Sundowner' F-8Ds were seen with *VF-26* and *USS Midway* titling on their starboard sides, retaining *VF-111* and *USS Kitty Hawk* markings to port. VF-111 headed for WestPac aboard CVA-63 the following month, however.

'Alfa Hotel 107' nicely framed by a photographer from an A-3, probably from CAG-11's VAH-13. The date is December 1963 – the same month the US Navy changed air group designations to air wings (*via Tailhook Association*)

VIETNAM

I n May 1964 American reconnaissance aircraft began Operation *Yankee Team* surveillance flights over Laos – especially the Plain of Jars. The 'Sundowners'' CO, Cdr Charles E Ray, provided single Crusaders to escort the photo aircraft. The operation was run from Washington, D.C., being controlled by the State Department and Department of Defense. Secretary of Defense Robert Strange McNamara had dictated a flight schedule of every other day at 1300 hrs local time, which of course solved many of the communist AA gunners' problems when it came to targeting the unarmed reconnaissance jets.

On 6 June Lt Charles F Klusmann of VFP-63 launched from *Kitty Hawk* and headed for the *Plaine des Jarres*. His Crusader had sustained AAA damage on a previous mission, but he had returned to 'the Kitty Boat'. This time he was not so fortunate, as his jet was struck by a 37 mm round at 2500 ft and he ejected, sustaining an ankle injury upon landing.

Pre-positioned CIA ('Air America') helicopters attempted to rescue the downed aviator but they were driven back by Pathet Lao gunfire with two crewmen wounded. Consequently, Klusmann was captured and held for 11 weeks before escaping in late August.

The next day VF-111's executive officer Cdr Doyle W Lynn drew a photo-escort mission, flying beneath a 4000-ft overcast. During the 450-knot photo run his Crusader was hit by automatic weapons. He lost both hydraulic control systems, leading to control failure. When the F-8 pitched nose-up, Lynn ejected safely from NH 101 (BuNo 147064). After hiding overnight, he was picked up by an 'Air America' helicopter. Thus began the US Navy's air war over Southeast Asia.

Following the Tonkin Gulf incident in August 1964, US forces were increasingly committed to Southeast Asia. Cdr James D LaHaye led

These four Crusaders flying from *Kitty Hawk* in 1964 had a long war ahead of them. However, they all survived combat, although NH 114 (BuNo 148699), which was upgraded into an F-8H, was subsequently destroyed in an accident with VF-124 – the Crusader fleet replacement squadron or 'RAG' – at NAS Miramar in 1970 (*via Tailhook Association*)

A *Midway* flightdeck crewman gets a close-up view as NH 452 (BuNo 147056) catches a wire during 1965 Tonkin Gulf operations (*via Tailhook Association*)

VF-111's 1965 deployment, flying F-8Ds in CVW-2 aboard *Midway*. LaHaye was an experienced Crusader pilot, having ejected from a VF-32 aircraft in 1958. In a typical air wing composition of the period, VF-111's Crusaders were teamed with VF-21's F-4B Phantom IIs. The deployment was a long one, extending from early March to late November, and it incurred significant losses – 17 in combat and five in accidents, resulting in 12 airmen being killed and five captured.

On 5 May Cdr LaHaye participated in an attack on Vinh airfield, flying NE 451 (BuNo 148637). Armed with Zuni rockets and 20 mm cannon, he rolled in to suppress North Vietnamese gunners, but 37 mm AAA struck hard. The skipper radioed, 'I've been hit! Have fire

A *Midway* 'red shirt' ordnanceman checks rockets on NE 456 before launch against targets in South Vietnam during the 1965 deployment (*via Tailhook Association*)

NE 452 (BuNo 147056) making a low-level attack, pulling 'streamers' from its wingtips in the humid atmosphere of South Vietnam. CVW-2 began its 1965 deployment with 'warm-up' strikes from 'Dixie Station' before *Midway* steamed north to operate on 'Yankee Station' (*via Tailhook Association*)

The same Crusader fires Zuni rockets. The 5-in (127 mm) diameter, folding-fin projectile was powered by a solid propellant motor with a burn time of roughly 1.3 seconds. The warhead could be variously armed for fragmentation, anti-tank or smoke, and it could weigh in at up to 45 lbs (*via Tailhook Association*)

warning light!' Streaming fuel, the stricken Crusader turned eastward for the Gulf of Tonkin. Other 'Sundowners' watched the CO descending wings level until he hit the water. There was no apparent reason for LaHaye's failure to eject, some speculating that his seat had suffered a malfunction.

LaHaye was succeeded as 'Old Nick One' by executive officer Doyle Lynn, who had survived his shootdown over Laos 11 months before. Actually, Lynn did not have to remain aboard *Midway* for he had received orders rotating him out of the squadron, but he elected to fill LaHaye's spot rather than have a new CO transferred in. However, VF-111's Vinh jinx struck again less than three weeks later when, on 27 May, Lynn was lost with BuNo 148706. He had led a flak-suppression section for a strike on the town's railway yard, but was struck by AAA. He called, 'I'm hit!', then his Crusader spun into the ground. No smoke or flame was seen, prompting the assumption that Lynn had been incapacitated in the cockpit, and therefore unable to eject.

Losing two COs in 19 days was a grim experience for any squadron. It would continue over the next seven years, as naval aviation lost scores of air wing, squadron and division leaders. Following Lynn's death, Cdr Dempsey Butler Jr moved in to command the 'Sundowners' for the rest of the year.

In June CVW-2 recorded the US Navy's first MiG kills of the Vietnam War, two by VF-21 F-4B Phantom IIs on the 17th and one by a VA-25 A-1H Skyraider on the 20th. The F-8s were denied any decisive MiG engagements, however.

VF-111's attrition continued when Lt(jg) G R Gollahan was killed by AAA on 12 August in BuNo 147911. On 3 November, CVW-2 suffered its final loss, albeit in a non-combat related incident, when the unnamed pilot of VF-111 jet BuNo 148635 suffered a control systems failure during an attack mission and he successfully ejected.

ORISKANY 1966

If the 1965 cruise was bad, the 1966 deployment was far worse. VF-111 was needed aboard USS *Oriskany* (CVA-34) with CVW-16 under Cdr Rodney B Carter. The 'O-Boat' was a veteran carrier, having logged nine deployments since 1951. On the 1965 cruise the air wing had included F-8E-equipped VMFA(AW)-212, which was replaced in 1966 by the 'Sundowners', led by Cdr Richard M Cook. Its sister squadron was VF-162, also flying F-8Es.

After the relative luxury of flying from a *Midway* class big deck carrier, the 'Sundowners' readjusted to the more demanding environment of a '27 Charlie' (a modified *Essex*-class ship). During pre-deployment training on 6 April Lt Cdr Norman Levy safely ejected from BuNo 150296. He returned to the squadron in ample time for the May departure to the Tonkin Gulf.

Lt(jg) Cody A Balisteri was flying a coastal armed reconnaissance on 11 August. Making 375 knots at 1800 ft, 'Old Nick 112' (BuNo 150880) was fired upon ten miles south of Hon Gay. Balisteri broke hard left, taking hits, and reported a depressing litany of problems – speed brake, hydraulic, oil and fire warning lights. With the F-8E vibrating badly it began an uncommanded right-hand roll. Balisteri made it 'feet wet' before ejecting over some offshore islands. He had lost, or abandoned, his flotation device and liferaft, and waited at the bottom of a 400-ft slope. An SH-3 'Big Mother' helicopter located him and put a rescue crewman ashore with a raft. The two men paddled beyond the breakers, where Lt Cdr R D Nichols had landed the Sea King because the rescue hoist had jammed. Balisteri returned to the squadron but died in the *Oriskany* fire two months later.

Two weeks after Balisteri's shootdown, Lt(jg) H J Meadows' AH 101 (BuNo 150907) sustained engine failure during a 23 August barrier CAP. He already knew the escape procedure, having ejected from an F-11A while a student aviator in 1964.

Oriskany's Crusaders logged some inconclusive MiG engagements during August, but the next month sustained a rare F-8 air-to-air loss. On 5 September the 'Sundowners' provided four Target Combat Air Patrol (TarCAP) fighters during an attack on enemy transport targets near Phy Ly. Leading the first pair

Amid the steam of the previous launch, *Midway* plane directors guide the pilot of NE 459 onto the catapult during 1965 operations in the Tonkin Gulf (*via Tailhook Association*)

A 'Sundowners' section of F-8Ds over California. NH 114 (BuNo 148699) and 'Triple sticks' NH 111 (BuNo 148638) were both converted to F-8H status and lost while flying with VF-124 in March and September 1970 (*via Tailhook Association*)

'Old Nick 112' on *Oriskany's* starboard catapult, ready to launch during the 1966 deployment. Note the *Sundowners* titling in white painted on the Insignia Red portion of the raised wing. (*via Mike O'Connor*)

was Lt Cdr Foster Teague, an extraordinarily colourful character who would feature prominently in several VF-111 actions. The second section was led by Capt Wilfred K Abbott, a USAF exchange pilot who had been flying since 1958.

Teague took his wingman inland to cover the Skyhawks, leaving Abbott and Lt Randy Rime to orbit offshore. When Teague reached minimum fuel level he egressed, allowing Abbott to head in and continue protecting the A-4s. A cloud layer forced Rime to fall in trail behind Abbott, reducing situational awareness. Circling at about 6000 ft, Abbott and Rime were surprised by a pair of MiG-17s emerging from the clouds. The 'Red Bandits' got within gunnery range without being spotted, hitting Rime's Crusader with 23 mm cannon rounds. Abbott pitched up to cover Rime, accepting a 90-degree shot from the stalkers. He placed his hope in the difficult gunnery problem – a close-range, high-deflection shot. Unfortunately for the USAF pilot, his North Vietnamese opponents could shoot.

The Crusader took multiple hits that proved devastating. Abbot's canopy was shattered, his instrument panel smashed and his helmet was knocked off. With the controls unresponsive, Abbott pulled the black and yellow handle, rocketing himself out of the doomed Vought. He parachuted into seven years of captivity, the 'Sundowners'' only jet loss to enemy aircraft.

Randy Rime barely escaped. Slightly wounded by glass splinters from his canopy, he evaded his assailants and just had sufficient fuel to limp back to the 'O-Boat'. He ignored the wave-off lights, caught a late wire and his starboard wheel fell off. Rime had about 300 lbs of JP-5 remaining – not enough for another pass at the deck.

Subsequently, *Oriskany* checked with the controllers responsible for monitoring enemy radio nets and tracking hostile aircraft. It became

The 'Sundowners' embarked in *Oriskany* on both the 1966 and 1967 cruises. CVW-16 sustained some of the heaviest losses of the Vietnam War, especially in 1966 when a disastrous shipboard fire killed 44 men (*via Tailhook Association*)

evident that the two MiGs had made a mess of a previous pass at the F-8s and then been directed to reposition for the successful bounce. For reasons never determined, Abbott and Rime had been denied this critical information. Abbott later recalled;

'On 5 September I was flying my F-8 Crusader in bright and sunny conditions when I was shot down over North Vietnam. In the ejection my right leg was broken. After the leg was finally operated on, I was in a cast for about four months. It took about two years, with my roommates' help, for me to achieve full use of the leg. It was my constant desire not to be a cripple so as to fly again someday. Other than my leg, the treatment and daily routine as a PoW was similar to that described by most other veterans. The food was just enough to sustain life. A constant battle was to keep our minds active. In the early years communication was extremely limited, but in the last couple of years we were able to conduct our own educational programmes – courses in everything from languages and mathematics to meat cutting, duplicate bridge and Toastmasters.'

Abbott may have fallen victim to North Vietnam's first ace, Nguyen Van Bay, who had already been involved in the downing of two Crusaders – an RF-8A and an F-8E off USS *Hancock* (CVA-19) on 21 June 1966. Later that month he claimed an F-105 and an A-4 (not confirmed by US records), adding four more victories in April 1967. Van Bay was, therefore, one of just four Vietnamese Peoples' Air Force (VPAF) MiG-17 pilots who probably participated in downing five or more American aircraft.

Oriskany gained retribution on 9 October when VF-162's Cdr Richard Bellinger bagged a MiG-21 – the first claimed by US Navy fighters.

On the morning of 26 October 1966, CVW-16 was preparing for another day of operations as ordnancemen downloaded flares from attack aircraft that had not been launched the night before.

Briefing for a 1966 mission from USS *Oriskany*. These pilots are, from left to right, Dick Schaffert, Jay Meadows, Pete Peters (standing), Bob Pearl, Bob Rasmussen (back row) and John Sande (*via Richard Schaffert*)

However, not all sailors were qualified for the task. Two inexperienced men accidentally activated a flare, and rather than tossing it overboard before it ignited, they threw it into an ordnance locker with hundreds of other flares. The result was a catastrophic fire that ultimately became one of the worst disasters in naval aviation history.

No fewer than 44 *Oriskany* men died in the conflagration, including CAG Rod Carter and 27 others from the air wing. Three 'Sundowners' perished. Lt Cdr Norman Levy was overcome by smoke while trying to obtain an oxygen breathing apparatus from a locker – he had survived ejections in April and August. Likewise, Lt(jg) Cody Balisteri had been rescued after his shootdown in August – he intended to enter medical school. Lt(jg) William G McWilliams (usually listed with VF-162) was the squadron's third loss.

Thirty-seven aircraft were destroyed or damaged beyond repair. However, the ship returned to California and, fully repaired and re-staffed, deployed again eight months later.

The next *Oriskany* deployment lasted seven months, from June 1967 to January 1968, and once more VF-111 (now flying F-8Cs) was heavily engaged. Cdr Robert L Rasmussen, a *Blue Angel* of 1957 vintage, assumed command two weeks before deploying. In a sign of the times, his pilots included three ensigns – a rarity explained by then Lt Cdr Richard Schaffert;

'The US Navy was running out of fighter pilots, and we were getting them straight from the training command with minimum hours. John Laughter was awarded the Distinguished Flying Cross for a mission during which he also logged his 100th hour in the Crusader! Absolutely crazy.'

The other ensigns selected by Rasmussen from VF-124 (the F-8 training squadron) were David Matheny and 22-year-old Tom Garrett. Matheny had 400 hours of flight time, including 190 in Crusaders.

On 31 July Lt Charles P Zuhoski's AH 110 (BuNo 146984) was destroyed by a SAM 20 miles southeast of Hanoi. Another 'new guy', he had received his wings in August 1966. After only four months in the squadron and two weeks in combat, a long war stretched before him as a PoW. Subsequently, Zuhoski said, 'The initial processing of me was speedy. I had been shot down and captured at about 0815 hrs, and I guess I was in "New Guy Village" learning the ropes by 1030 hrs

The 'Sundowners' aboard *Oriskany* in October 1967. Standing in the back row, from left to right, are CO Bob Rasmussen, Jake Jacobsen, Craig Taylor, Don Baker, Tom Garrett, Pete Peters (Maintenance Officer), Carl Stattin and XO Jack Finney. In the front row, from left to right, are Dick Schaffert (Ops Officer), Al Aston, Bob Jurgens, John Laughter, Jay Meadows, John Sande and USAF exchange pilot Capt Andy Anderson (*via Richard Schaffert*)

Briefing in *Oriskany's* Ready Room Three on 5 October 1967. From left right are Dave Matheny (shot down and captured on this mission), John Laughter, Dick Schaffert, Bob Rasmussen (back of head) and Don Baker (spare, did not launch). Schaffert briefed the TarCAP flight and flew with Laughter. Rasmussen led the strike escort with Matheny on his wing (*via Richard Schaffert*)

on the 31st. I was a PoW for five years and seven months. I consider myself lucky for I was not singled out during hard times as many of the PoWs were'.

The next loss occurred on 8 September when Lt Cdr Donald Baker's Crusader (BuNo 146929) was badly damaged by ground fire. The Naval Aviator managed to make it back to the task force, but lacking enough fuel to get aboard *Oriskany*, he ejected and was soon rescued. Because Baker returned to the carrier his aircraft was logged as an 'operational' loss.

One of the squadron's 'nuggets' was lost on 5 October when 23-year-old Ens David P Matheny was hit by AAA while attacking a pontoon bridge ten miles west of Phat Diem, near the border of Thanh Hoa and Ninh Binh Provinces. Making 450 knots at 400 ft, he was tagged by flak – probably 37 mm cannon rounds. With an intermittent fire, Matheny turned toward a designated bailout area and safely ejected from 'Old Nick 114' (BuNo 146938). Although first listed as missing in action, on 2 January 1968 his status was changed to captured. The next month he and two USAF pilots were handed over to anti-war Catholic priests. Matheny's exceptional memory allowed him to return with the names of about 260 prisoners, some of whom had been listed as missing up until then.

The 'Sundowners' suffered an operational loss on 19 November when Lt Edward W Van Orden was killed in AH 102 (BuNo 147004). The Crusader crashed on launch, and Van Orden had no chance to eject.

VF-111's final loss of the year came on 5 December when Lt Jay Meadows, who had ejected in August 1966, was downed by AAA. Escorting a photo-reconnaissance Crusader near Vinh at 1500 ft, he was fired upon by automatic weapons. Meadows felt a vibration in his F-8C, then noted a fire warning light followed by loss of his primary control system. The pilot of the RF-8 then got on the radio and told him that 'Old Nick 102' (BuNo 146907) was bleeding hydraulic fluid. Turning seaward, the Crusaders made for the southern search and rescue (SAR) station, but when approaching the destroyer Meadows

VF-111 operations officer Lt Cdr Richard 'Brown Bear' Schaffert on 24 October 1967, before the first of six missions against the Hanoi area in four days. He fought a single-handed battle against four MiG-17s on 14 December 1967, successfully defending an 'Iron Hand' A-4 Skyhawk on the same day that the 'Sundowners'' sister squadron, VF-162, downed another MiG (*via Richard Schaffert*)

felt an explosion and lost all remaining control pressure. Out of options, he parachuted into the Tonkin Gulf and was quickly rescued. It was the third ejection of his career.

THE SAGA OF 'BROWN BEAR'

One of the highlights of the 1967 cruise was a fighter combat that did not result in a MiG kill. Nevertheless, it entered legend as one of the classic dogfights of the jet age.

On the afternoon of 14 December, Lt Cdr Dick Schaffert escorted an A-4E on an *Iron Hand* anti-SAM (surface-to-air missile) mission supporting a mining operation between Hanoi and Haiphong. Alerted by bandit calls, 'Brown Bear' Schaffert remained vigilant while the Skyhawk pilot, Lt(jg) Charles Nelson, prepared to fire an AGM-45 Shrike anti-radar missile. At that moment Schaffert spied a glint – two MiG-17s. He called Nelson, who also spotted the threat, but lost sight of the Crusader.

Schaffert rolled in from his 18,000-ft perch, tracking the MiG section as he descended. Pulling level at 3000 ft, he looked for Nelson . . . and saw two more MiGs. Schaffert laid the control column over and pulled hard, loading eight Gs on 'Old Nick 106'. 'Brown Bear' had 3500 hours of fighter time, and he would need all of that experience to survive on the short end of four-to-one odds.

Schaffert's initial break forced the nearest MiGs to overshoot, but the exceptional stress pulled his oxygen mask below his chin. Unable to call for help, he was on his own.

It was nearly impossible for a Crusader to turn with a MiG-17 so Schaffert did what F-8 pilots did best – he fought in the vertical. Kicking in and out of afterburner, he began a series of 'yo-yo' manoeuvres peaking as high as 25,000 ft, trying to deny the VPAF pilots a good shot at him, while striving for an advantageous position. The odds against Schaffert were improved since the four MiGs fought as two sections, permitting the former tactics instructor to conduct the engagement as a '1-v-2'.

The first time Schaffert got a tracking tone from one of his Sidewinders, he was about to shoot when 23 mm tracers flashed past his canopy. The second pair had quickly reversed and countered his run on the first section. After three more 'yo-yos', Schaffert had worked into position for a missile shot, but the AIM-9B passed between two MiGs without exploding. One of his four Sidewinders had been inoperative before launch, so he was now left with just two missiles.

Working hard, timing his breaks and pitch-ups, Schaffert sustained high-G overhead reversals to defeat the MiGs' superior turning radius. The next time he pressed the trigger, the missile tracked but failed to explode. In turn, two MiGs fired 'Atoll' heat-seeking missiles at the F-8 but the launches were out of parameter. Schaffert's third Sidewinder failed to guide. He was beyond frustration – three good shots and three malfunctions. But 'Brown Bear' was undaunted. With hundreds of gunnery flights in his logbook, he felt confident that he could hit anything in range. When a MiG presented him with a tracking solution, Schaffert pulled into a five-G turn and, at a range of 800 ft, pressed the trigger. All four 20 mm cannon choked. The high-G manoeuvres had disconnected the pneumatic ammunition feed system!

At some point in the fight two MiG-21s blazed through the combat area, firing 'Atolls'. Schaffert was barely aware of them.

Nonetheless, Schaffert determined to teach the Vietnamese a lesson. Still feeling confident, he pulled into another high-altitude yo-yo, engaging in a vertical rolling scissors with the enemy leader. At the bottom of that evolution Schaffert bent the throttle for the coast, leaving the MiGs behind. He recovered aboard *Oriskany* with merely 200 lbs of JP-5 remaining. There, VF-162 skipper Cdr Cal Swanson and Lt Richard

A January 1968 awards ceremony at NAS Miramar featured two generations of 'Sundowners'. Left to right are VF-111 executive officer Cdr Jack Finney, Rear Adm Gene Fairfax (VF-11 CO in 1944) and Lt Cdr Dick Schaffert (*via Richard Schaffert*)

Wyman performed a victory roll after the latter had successfully engaged another MiG-17. Schaffert had survived a gruelling ten-minute solo combat with six MiGs – a classic engagement still examined at Topgun decades later. He recalled, 'I needed every ounce of experience to come away from that mission intact'. Schaffert's 1500 hours in F-8s had been time well spent.

'Old Nick 106' was Schaffert's lucky aeroplane. He flew it five times during the 1967 cruise and saw MiGs on three occasions. 'Only two days after the 14 December fight, John Sande and I chased two MiG-21s back to Hanoi while capping for Brian Compton (commanding VA-163) on another strike in the "Hour Glass" – same area as the fight', Schaffert explained.

The 'Sundowners' logged carrier aviation's first loss of the new year when, on 2 January 1968, Lt(jg) Craig M Taylor was assigned a photo escort mission to Dong Phong Thuong, northeast of Thanh Hoa. Flying through heavy-calibre flak at 5000 ft, BuNo 146989 sustained AAA damage leading to partial loss of power, then complete electrical failure. Taylor had to put the nose down to maintain airspeed while

A section of 'Sundowner' Crusaders tank from 'buddy packs' provided by VA-164 Skyhawks. Note the F-8s' full air-to-air loadout with two AIM-9 Sidewinders on each side. 'Old Nick 106' (BuNo 146989) in the foreground fell to AAA on 2 January 1968 but Lt(jg) Craig Taylor survived (*via Tailhook Association*)

egressing over the coast, staying with the dying F-8 for as long as possible. When it stalled, he punched out at 800 ft. Despite landing amid Vietnamese fishing vessels, Taylor was retrieved by a SAR SH-3.

'OMAR'S ORPHINS' – *INTREPID* 1967-68

While CVW-16 set out again in *Oriskany*, the 'Sundowners' were also employed elsewhere. A new concept involving attack squadrons embarked in antisubmarine carriers (reclassified as limited capability attack carriers) had seen USS *Intrepid* (CVS-11) embark CVW-10 – and its A-1 and A-4 squadrons – for its 1966 Vietnam cruise. In fact, a VA-176 Skyraider flying from the vessel had shot down a MiG-17 on 9 October 1966.

For the 1967 deployment *Intrepid* operated a reorganised CVW-10 with three A-4 Skyhawk squadrons and an A-1 Skyraider unit, plus 'cats and dogs' for reconnaissance, early warning and jamming. Therefore, the requirement for a fighter escort for the RF-8s of VFP-63 Det 11 led to a three-aeroplane detachment called 'Omar's Orphans'. Deploying between May and December, 'Sundowner' Det 11's officer in charge was the colourful, capable Lt Cdr Foster S Teague.

'Tooter' Teague was a strapping Louisianan who had been flying fighters since 1958. He joined VF-111 in 1966 and immediately made an impression. One squadronmate described him as 'the bravest guy I ever met. A great guy to go on liberty with, but very professional when it came to the squadron'.

With *Intrepid's* cobbled-together air wing, space came at a premium. The 'Sundowners' shared Ready Room One with VSF-3, the A-4B squadron doubling as fighters, as its jets were capable of firing AIM-9s. Because the 'Chessmen' had an 'F' in their designation, requiring quick access to the flightdeck, they claimed the largest ready room. Even so, the 16 Skyhawk and four Crusader pilots lived cheek by jowl. As one Naval Aviator from VSF-3 recalled, 'The seats on the other side of aisle were theirs. Flight gear and coffee mess were shared. Crowded as hell'.

The various squadrons' LSOs had only 'waved' A-4s and piston-engined aircraft in the past, so adjusting to F-8s posed a major challenge. Fortunately, the two air wing LSOs had experience with 'the steel dart' and worked well with Teague's pilots.

On 9 July 1967 the 'Sundowners' took the war to the enemy's home nest. Teague had a 'nugget' wingman, Lt(jg) Joseph 'Roadrunner' Satrapa, who was undertaking his first combat deployment. Satrapa was a big, cheerful Californian with a powerful, competitive spirit. Academically he had finished 926th of 927 in the Annapolis class of 1964, but his contemporaries said nobody possessed more of a warrior ethic. MiG killer John 'Pirate' Nichols said '"Satrapa Joe" was the kind of man you wanted with you in a gunfight'.

In fact, guns and explosives were of special interest to Satrapa. He was known for his arsenal of firearms, including pistols and revolvers, and even a 'chopped' Thompson sub-machine gun. Satrapa had traded a leather flight jacket with some Marines for a case of grenades, and reportedly carried two 'pineapples' on his torso harness in case he was downed. Later, as a tactics instructor, Satrapa insisted, 'Just because you're on the ground doesn't mean the fight's over'.

While *Intrepid* Skyhawks egressed from targets north of Phuc Yen airfield, Teague noticed activity on the MiG base. He nosed over, lined up a row of MiG-17s and opened fire. Satrapa, previously focused on keeping formation, was astonished with the view through his windscreen. He saw Teague's 20 mm shells ignite one parked fighter, then strike another. Satrapa figured he might as well join in and contributed some of his own ammunition. Then the F-8s were past the airfield perimeter, heading for the Tonkin Gulf. Back aboard *Intrepid,* Teague advised his young partner that it might be best to avoid mentioning the episode.

On 31 July Lt(jg) Charles P Zuhoski was escorting A-4s against a SAM site near Hanoi when the defenders fired multiple SA-2s. While jinking at about 11,000 ft Zuhoski's F-8C (BuNo 146984) was struck by a missile that hit the rear fuselage. His engine immediately seized and the Crusader burst into flames. Zuhoski ejected at about 350 knots and spent the next five-and-a-half years in captivity.

As if in revenge for the insult for 9 July, North Vietnamese AAA gunners shot down 'Tooter' Teague on 12 August. Flying a TarCAP near the Ke Sat highway bridge, his flight drew SA-2 SAMs, prompting evasive action that depleted much of his energy. Teague was down to 230 knots at only 2000 ft, making a hard right turn, when 'Old Nick 17' (BuNo 146993) was hit by gunfire. Two minutes later his wingman called that the Crusader was streaming hydraulic fluid, and Teague got a fire warning light as his secondary control system failed. He resorted to desperate measures, twice shutting down the J57 in an attempt to extinguish the fire, but each time the flames resumed.

During the 1967 *Intrepid* deployment Lt(jg) Tony Nargi's assigned aircraft was AK 17, here with an unidentified pilot following instructions from the plane directors. The F-8C (BuNo 146993) was shot down on 9 July, with Lt Cdr F S Teague ejecting safely (*via Mike O'Connor*)

Teague then felt 'a definite explosion within the aircraft', and the control column went fully forward. Out of options, he pulled the handle and ejected.

Teague's canopy opened safely, but during the descent he felt himself slipping out of his torso harness. The model then in use was ill suited to a tropical climate, prompting many pilots to cut away straps and material that retained heat. Teague had trimmed his harness too much and now risked plummeting from a fatal height. However, by hugging himself tightly he remained in the harness, and safely dropped into the water. Rescued by a US Navy helicopter, he was returned to *Intrepid*.

Near the end of the cruise Teague offered an A-4 pilot the chance to fly a Crusader. Lt R R 'Boom' Powell leapt at the opportunity and learned the cockpit procedures while an F-8 sat on deck. The plan was for Powell to launch from *Intrepid* and land ashore at Cubi Point, in the Philippines. However, at the last moment orders came down to send the F-8s to *Oriskany*. 'There went my chance at Crusader glory', Powell lamented. 'But "Tooter" was a great guy. You'd probably go to prison for doing something like that today!'

Intrepid returned home in time for Christmas, but another combat deployment lay just over the horizon.

Once again 'Omar's Orphans' were assigned to *Intrepid*, scheduled to deploy in June 1968. One aircraft was lost before deployment when Lt Anthony J Nargi ejected from BuNo 147026 on 6 May.

As before, Det 11 was loaded with talent. Lt Cdr William K 'Dusty' Rhodes was already well known in fighter circles, and his roster included some of the most aggressively capable warriors in the business. Lt(jg) Alexander Rucker said, 'We had great rapport with the ship's company and the rest of the air wing. We were seen as gods almost – it was embarrassing – but our status as fighter pilots was some kind of magic'. All the magicians needed was a chance.

On 1 August 1968 two 'Sundowners' engaged MiGs. The section was led by Tony Nargi, trailing a VF-51 flight off *Bon Homme Richard*. The Crusader pilots found MiG-21s near Vinh, in the southern part of North Vietnam, and each section alternated pressing the fight. In the early phase the 'Bonny Dick' pilots fired three Sidewinders without effect. Covered by Lt(jg) Carl Orlob, Nargi then engaged a MiG in a tight manoeuvring duel and closed to gun range. He fired and saw pieces fly off the MiG-21, which broke for a nearby cloud. To avoid an overshoot, Nargi deployed his speed brakes, chopped the throttle to idle and joined on the MiG 'in close parade formation'. He could see his opponent, who apparently did not notice him before entering the cloud. As they emerged, the VPAF pilot finally spotted the F-8 to starboard and

Lt Cdr W K Rhodes' *Intrepid* **detachment prior to departing Miramar for the East Coast, circa April 1968. In the front row, from left to right, are Frank Corah, Carl Orlob, Rick Wenzel and Alex Rucker. And in the back row, from left to right, are Walt Smith (maintenance officer), Joe Thompson, 'Dusty' Rhodes, Tony Nargi and Joe Satrapa** (*via Alex Rucker*)

broke left. Nargi was lagging the bandit, striving for nose-to-tail separation that would permit a minimum-range Sidewinder shot.

The VF-51 leader, Lt Norman McCoy, was waiting from a perch for the MiG to exit the far side of the cloud. He saw Nargi pulling away for separation and dropped down to re-attack the MiG. When it broke right, McCoy gained a favourable aspect. He pulled lead and fired – the missile destroyed the MiG-21 in a large fireball. Unseen by the Americans, the Vietnamese pilot ejected. In 2005 McCoy learned that 'his' MiG pilot was killed in combat with Phantom IIs off USS *Constellation* (CVA-64) in May 1972.

Knowing that McCoy and his wingman would be low on fuel, Nargi covered them en route to a tanker. It was a case of 'second time unlucky' for Tony Nargi, who had pushed his fuel – and his orders – by pursuing MiGs into Chinese airspace during the 1967 deployment. On that occasion Nargi's wingman had been the combative 'Roadrunner' (later 'Hoser') Satrapa. Less than a week after McCoy's success, Satrapa got another chance to put the 'Sundowners' on the scoreboard.

On 7 August Satrapa flew a MiGCAP with Alex Rucker. 'Rattler' was an enthusiastic pilot with 160 hours in F-8s. He had considered Marine Corps aviation but never even glanced at the USAF. He was especially glad of the Det 11 assignment since his brother Bill was an *Intrepid* communications officer.

Portrait of a warrior. Lt(jg) Joseph Satrapa manning up during the *Intrepid* cruise of 1968. A colourful character in a colourful crew, 'Roadrunner' later changed his callsign to 'Hoser' owing to his fondness for aerial gunnery and all manner of firearms (*via Alex Rucker*)

Offshore near Vinh, the VF-111 section was alerted to possible MiGs by the radar-control ship, and headed inland. At that moment Rucker's radio failed. He signalled loss of communication and, in an unorthodox measure, Satrapa used his hand-held emergency radio to transmit to his wingman. Going 'feet wet' without full 'comm' was contrary to regulations and good sense, so Satrapa had Rucker orbit offshore while he continued the pursuit. Accelerating in afterburner, Satrapa began eating up the distance to the MiGs. However, a quick glance in his rear-view mirror showed Rucker faithfully following. Rather than expose 'Rattler' to unnecessary risk, 'Roadrunner' broke off the chase and duly returned to *Intrepid*.

On 18 September VF-111 launched two F-8Cs on TarCAP west of Vinh Son. The leader was Lt Frank Corah and his wingman Alex Rucker, who had flown with Joe Satrapa in the abortive chase in August. As Rucker related;

'Frank had the lead when I spotted the black delta planform (slightly to starboard) silhouetted against a humongous thunderstorm. It was probably five miles away or more. I called the bogey out to Frank and, since I was "padlocked" and he didn't have the bogey in sight, he passed the lead to me. We pursued the MiG until we lost sight of him as he flew around to the opposite side of the storm.'

It was another frustrating outcome for aggressive aviators, as US Navy fighters claimed only nine MiG victories in 1968 – half the previous year's toll. But Crusaders notched five of the kills, the last being a 'Sundowner' victory.

The day after the fruitless MiG-21 sighting, Rucker got another chance. On 19 September he was wingman to Tony Nargi, 28-year-old alumnus of the Annapolis class of 1963. Flying his third Vietnam tour, Nargi was a veteran of two other F-8 squadrons. He had survived the 1966 *Oriskany* cruise with its fatal fire, and leapt at the chance to join 'Tooter' Teague in *Intrepid*.

After providing TarCAP for a strike, the F-8s hooked up to a tanker over the Tonkin Gulf, then reported to the controller. The 'Sundowners' were directed to a position with another Crusader duo from *Bon Homme Richard*. Shortly after 1700 hrs the controlling ship, USS *Long Beach* (CGN-9), alerted the fighters to bogies, then sent the F-8s on a northwesterly heading. Flying 'Old Nick 103' (BuNo 146961), Nargi gave the lead to a VF-211 section, led by Lt Patrick Scott. Going feet dry at Vinh – scene of many a MiG encounter – the Crusaders learned of another radar contact to the west. The F-8s were told to orbit until the radar picture clarified, but at that point Scott had radio and compass problems. Nargi compensated by passing *Long Beach's* information to him, but almost immediately a bandit was on them. Nargi called, 'Tally ho! MiG-21. High'. Nargi and Rucker lit their afterburners, gaining energy for the inevitable manoeuvring to come.

The 'Checkertail' pilots had not seen the MiG and turned left, allowing the 'Sundowners' to engage. The MiG-21 entered a looping manoeuvre, with Rucker off Nargi's port wing. On the down slope the bandit turned right, allowing his pursuers to cut the corner and close the distance. Evidently disoriented, the VPAF pilot levelled off briefly, then made a shallow left turn. The aspect was nearly ideal for a Sidewinder shot – Nargi pressed the trigger at less than a mile. Slightly above, Rucker had a beautiful view of the missile strike. He thought the AIM-9 flew directly into the MiG's engine, exploding in an orange fireball. Instantly the canopy flew off and the seat left the aircraft. The defeated enemy pilot dangled beneath an orange and white parachute.

Lt Tony Nargi and Lt(jg) Alex Rucker with *Intrepid's* executive officer, Cdr T D Brown, after their successful MiG engagement on 19 September 1968. This was the carrier's second, and last, aerial victory of the Vietnam War. It was also the last for the F-8 Crusader (*via Mike O'Connor*)

MiG killer! 'Old Nick 103' was the assigned aircraft of Lt Joe Thompson, hence the 'Tiger' callsign on the tail stripe. But BuNo 146961 was flown by Tony Nargi in making his MiG-21 kill during 'Omar's Orphans'' detachment aboard *Intrepid* in 1968 (*via Tailhook Association*)

At that moment Rucker wondered about the MiG's likely wingman. Checking his tail, 'Rattler' turned port to clear his rear hemisphere – and saw another MiG-21, 'bigger than life, about 2000 ft at our "six o'clock"'. There was also an 'Atoll' in the air. Rucker shouted for a right turn and saw the heat-seeker streak past both Crusaders. Seconds later their assailant also appeared ahead of the F-8s, unable to compensate for a very high overtaking speed. Seizing the momentary advantage, Nargi launched another AIM-9, which missed.

Not to be denied the rare opportunity, the VF-211 pilots jumped into the fight. Lt Leon Swaim fired his first Sidewinder well within parameters but the new MiG pilot saw the threat and abruptly pitched up, defeating the shot. Chased by four hungry Crusaders, the MiG then accelerated rapidly northward.

By then Nargi was out of Sidewinders, calling for someone else to take a shot. At perhaps two miles Rucker got an audible tone – proof that his missile was tracking a heat source – and fired. The weapon performed splendidly and, despite the long range, sped to the target and exploded. However, the MiG continued its headlong dash. At that point the 'Checkertail' leader, Lt Scott, took a turn. When the bandit broke left, Scott fired an AIM-9 that seemed to perform a roll around the intended victim. Having survived four missile shots, the VPAF pilot plunged into a cloud and escaped.

Back at the ship, Tony Nargi performed the traditional victory roll before entering the landing pattern. Both pilots 'boltered' (missed the arresting wire) on the first attempt, but got aboard the next time. As 'Rattler' Rucker said, 'The whole world was there to greet us!' Looking back on the cruise, he reflected, 'I thoroughly enjoyed the camaraderie and bon vivant lifestyle of being a fighter pilot in those heady days'.

VF-111 had scored the 19th, and last, F-8 victory. The cruise ended in February 1969, at which point 'Omar's Orphans' passed into history. They had been among the last carrier aviators in combat before President Lyndon Johnson's halted the bombing of most of North Vietnam. Lt Cdr Rhodes' detachment returned home just as the rest of VF-111 deployed in USS *Ticonderoga* (CVA-14). Coincidentally, 'Tico' was the 'Sundowners'' 14th carrier since the unit embarked in its sister ship *Hornet* in 1944-45. Cdr Jack L Finley led the squadron through the seven-month 1969 cruise with no combat losses.

During the *Ticonderoga* cruise (February to September 1969) President Richard Nixon authorised the bombing of communist bases

'The skipper's bird' is literally written all over AH 101. Photographed in 1968, BuNo 146991 has *CDR JACK FINNEY* painted beneath the cockpit plus classic 'Sundowners' markings in the form of the 'sharksmouth' and eyes around the intake. This jet was later upgraded to F-8K specification (*via Tailhook Association*)

Shangri-La took VF-111 on its longest deployment of the Vietnam War, the vessel being seen here at anchor in Wellington harbour, New Zealand, during that 1970 cruise (*via Tailhook Association*)

in Cambodia, but also announced the start of 'Vietnamization'. With the Saigon government pledged to take an increasing role in its own defence, 25,000 American troops were to be withdrawn almost immediately. But others remained at risk. On 6 July Lt G P Hahn's F-8H (BuNo 148636) sustained partial engine failure from loss of oil pressure. The engine would continue to run at 89 percent power, but when Hahn advanced the throttle to 91 percent it suffered total failure and he was forced to eject.

Following the 'Tico' cruise, Cdr Charles Dimon relieved Jack Finley in Hong Kong, then conducted the turnaround training phase. Thus began the squadron's longest deployment since World War 2 – more than nine months with CVW-8 in *Shangri-La*, departing in March 1970. The 'Sundowners' had flown Furies from 'Shang' in 1959, and in the interim it had been converted to an ASW carrier, but now deployed with a full attack air wing. However, the vessel's expected Mediterranean cruise was abruptly changed to WestPac, prompting some last-minute shuffling.

'Stinger' Dimon deployed with only seven pilots and four Crusaders, plus about half the 180 enlisted men as the carrier steamed round Cape Horn, bound for the Philippines. Meanwhile the executive officer, Cdr Bill Rennie, led the other eight jets and the balance of the personnel from Miramar to Cubi Point in April. Knowing that half the aviators were due to roll out, Dimon and Rennie had split the squadron so as to give the departing officers more time at home.

Despite the duration of the cruise, relatively little of note occurred in Southeast Asia in 1970. The main action began in April, when US and South Vietnamese troops advanced into Cambodia to dislodge North Vietnamese forces from the area.

When the air wing commander unexpectedly left the ship in June, Dimon filled in for two weeks until a replacement arrived. Rennie then assumed command of VF-111.

Some levity was injected into the 'Shang' cruise, notably by Lt James Best. 'Red' hailed from Tennessee, where he had paid the bills with his harmonica artistry. As he recalled it, 'BarCap would get a little boring at times, so I carried a harmonica (key of G) in my G-suit pocket and played some for my own entertainment until one day on north Tonkin CAP, I asked "Red Crown" if they could use a "harmonic check". The controller said he was open to anything, so I played *The Yellow Rose of Texas* and it hit a chord because he was from Texas.

'After that when the "Varmint Section" (I was "Red Fox" and Chuck Scott was "Coyote") checked in, we had a request for something already waiting. Lt Cdr Buddy Penn was an A-3 tanker driver and African-American pal of mine. He would ask for a song before I could get tanked. One day I moved into position for tanking and played *Old Black Joe,* to which he unceremoniously reeled in the drogue. Apology was accepted and I got my JP quota.'

Returning to California in December 1970, most of the 'Shang' squadrons found themselves facing extinction. It was a period of force reduction that hit CVW-8 especially hard. VF-162, VA-152 and VA-172 were quickly disestablished, and only VF-111 and VA-12 survived the attrition, the 'Sundowners' under Rennie, who turned over to Cdr Harlan R Pearl in June 1971.

CORAL SEA 1971-72

In early 1971 VF-111 traded in its beloved Crusaders after flying F-8s for almost a decade, transitioning to F-4B Phantom IIs. Simultaneously the 'Sundowners' were permanently assigned to CVW-15 – an affiliation that would endure for the remainder of their existence. The 1971-72 Vietnam cruise also began a 23-year association with VF-51. The partnership would remain intact over the next 13 deployments.

Having spent its entire career with single-seat fighters, VF-111 had to adjust to a wholly different mindset – two-seat, multi-mission aircraft. Despite the fighter pilot's jibe that he would rather have 200 lbs more fuel than a radar intercept officer (RIO), many Naval Aviators recognised the advantages. That second pair of eyes could pay huge dividends in combat, regardless of the Phantom II's powerful radar. No less an authority than 'Tooter' Teague (who later flew F-4Bs in VF-51) became a 'Phantom Phan'.

F-8H BuNo 147048 was AJ 00, flown by Cdr William Stollenwerck during the *Shangri-La* deployment of 1970. The multi-hued tail contains colours from each squadron in the wing – red for the 100 series, yellow for the 200s, blue for the 300s, orange for the 400s and green for 500. This fighter was lost while serving with a Marine Corps squadron in 1973 (*via Tailhook Association*)

During the *Coral Sea* deployment the 'air boss' was Cdr Chuck Dimon, 'Sundowners' skipper in 1969-70. He recalled, 'Pearl (CO of VF-111) and Teague (CO of VF-51) and everybody all wanted favours!'

When 'Coral Maru' steamed westbound in November 1971, its air wing expected another round of routine missions, mainly south of the DMZ. With the bombing halt approaching its fourth year, there was little reason to expect aerial opposition. The last MiG kills had been achieved by *Constellation* Phantom IIs in a rare encounter during March 1970. Some of Cdr Pearl's VF-111 crews had compared notes with returning *Midway* aviators who said that their 1971 deployment had been 'little more than a training exercise'. It was a disappointment to some enthusiastic 'Sundowners' like RIO Lt(jg) William Freckleton, who said 'I wanted a taste of combat since that's what I had been trained for'.

However, there were still perils to be faced in Southeast Asian skies – on 30 December 1971 the squadron lost 'Old Nick 203' (BuNo 150418). Flying near Vinh at 2000 ft, Lt Cdr David W Hoffman's F-4B took a SAM hit in the tail, the aircraft splashing offshore. Hoffman and Lt(jg) Norris A Charles were captured, although Charles was released eight months later. Their luck was notably poor, for BuNo 150418 was one of only four carrier aircraft lost in combat that year.

With American aircraft conducting increased 'Blue Tree' reconnaissance missions over North Vietnam, the MiGs became more active. The future ace team of Lt Randy Cunningham and Lt(jg) Willy Driscoll from *Constellation's* VF-96 broke the two-year famine by downing a MiG-21 on 19 January 1972.

Events accelerated on 6 March. *Coral Sea* reconnaissance pilots saw MiGs over Quang Lang airfield, and later that day VF-51 tangled with

F-4B BuNo 153019 was among the first 'Sundowners'' Phantom IIs obtained by the unit in August 1971. Given the modex NL 201, it was assigned to the CO, Cdr Harlan R Pearl, although no names have been applied to the canopy rails. This machine later became the unit's only MiG-killing Phantom II (*via Tailhook Association*)

Coral Sea's launch officer observed the 1971 Christmas season with suitable attire as NL 200 is readied on the port catapult somewhere in the South China Sea (*via Mike O'Connor*)

The team of Lt Garry Weigand and Lt(jg) Bill Freckleton scored VF-111's only Phantom II kill when they downed a MiG-17 on 6 March 1972. It was the 'Sundowners' 161st, and last, aerial victory in three wars (*via Mike O'Connor*)

bandits. The 'Screaming Eagles'' leader 'Tooter' Teague responded to radio calls of MiGs in the air, and when the enemy stayed to fight, he fired a Sidewinder that he thought connected. Post-strike reconnaissance showed the intended victim parked at Quang Lang, however – Teague got a confirmed kill in June.

The next launch also encountered MiGs, the two-aeroplane section being led by Lt Jim Stillinger with RIO Lt(jg) Rick Olin. The wingman was Lt Gary Weigand and Lt(jg) Bill Freckleton.

'Grayhound' Weigand, hailing from Virginia, had been fascinated with carrier aviation since childhood. Redheaded 'Farkle' Freckleton was a navy brat born in Scotland, and he had been teamed with Weigand since the end of 1970. Freckleton had 375 flying hours to his name, including 222 in F-4s. They were flying the CO's jet, NL 201 (BuNo 153019), which they had flown in six times previously.

The 'Sundowners' were assigned to patrol near Quang Lang, covering an RA-5C Vigilante sortie. However, neither Phantom II had an all-up radar system, and only the lead had a limited Sparrow capability. 'Old Nick 201' carried AIM-9D Sidewinders, which restricted Weigand to rear-hemisphere shots. The section had barely taken up its position when it received a 'heads up' call from the *Red Crown* radar controller offshore. Beginning at 15 miles, the range calls steadily diminished from the west. The final call placed bandits just two miles out.

Stillinger followed the controller's instructions, breaking down to port. He saw a MiG-17 perhaps 1000 ft off the ground, pointing its blunt nose at the lead Phantom II. In 'NL 201's' rear seat, with an inoperative radar, Freckleton immediately became a second set of eyes. He began searching visually, while Weigand pulled up to cover their leader from an altitude perch.

Manoeuvring with the green MiG, Stillinger used the F-4's vertical performance to 'yo-yo' against the enemy's superior turn radius. Finally, he got a favourable angle and launched an AIM-9 that the MiG avoided. From the initial merge it was apparent that the VPAF pilot was both capable and confident, and he showed no inclination to disengage.

Deciding to extend away from the threat, Stillinger called Weigand to roll in, keeping the pressure on the MiG. But the bandit was determined – he selected afterburner, attempting to reach gun range of Stillinger and Olin. As Weigand dived into the fight, he saw a favourable situation developing. The enemy's aggressiveness left him vulnerable to a 'six o'clock' attack, and 'Grayhound' seized the opportunity. With a good tone in his earphones he knew his first AIM-9 was tracking the MiG's exhaust. Simultaneously, Freckleton

NL 201 back at Miramar in late 1972, sporting a kill symbol for Weigand and Freckleton's MiG-17. A yellow VPAF star was painted above the black silhouette on the port splitter vane. This jet later went to Reserve unit VF-201 in the early 1980s and subsequently to VF-101 det Key West. Withdrawn from service in 1985, it is now a 'gate guard' at NAS Key West, Florida (*via Bill Freckleton*)

The communist 'Easter offensive' of 1972 prompted an end to the four-year bombing halt in most of North Vietnam. These *Coral Sea* F-4Bs are seen here releasing 500-lb Mk 82s on 8 March 1972. The nearest jet is 'Old Nick 204' (BuNo 150466), with VF-51's 'Screaming Eagle 113' (BuNo 149457) in the distance. The latter downed a MiG-17 on 11 June 1972 (*via Tailhook Association*)

was clearing their tail, hollering for his pilot to shoot. The Sidewinder flashed off the rail, tracked straight to the tailpipe and exploded. The MiG's tail was severed, sending the wreckage plummeting into the ground, where it erupted in a fireball. Senior Lieutenant Hoang Ioh died in his aircraft.

Now *Red Crown* was back on the air with chilling information – six MiG-21s were inbound, obviously keen on revenge. The two 'Sundowners' bent their throttles for the coast, accelerating away from the wall of MiGs rocketing toward them.

After refuelling from a KA-3 tanker the two Phantom IIs returned to 'Coral Maru', performing victory rolls overhead the vessel. The mission ended perfectly as both pilots snagged the number three wire for OK3 landings. A ready room party celebrated the 'Sundowners'' 161st, and final, aerial victory.

The communist 'Easter offensive' into South Vietnam broke the four-year deadlock following Lyndon Johnson's departure in 1968. Facing an all-out assault, South Vietnam badly needed American air power to punish Hanoi for its violation, and carrier aviation contributed heavily.

'Coral Maru' returned home in July 1972, having logged 148 days of combat operations. A negotiated ceasefire took effect in January 1973.

It had been a long war. During the course of seven Vietnam deployments VF-111 had logged 12,500 sorties, losing 20 jets in flight, four pilots killed in action, three killed during the *Oriskany* fire and five captured. However heavy the Vietnam casualties appeared, they could not match the scale of World War 2. In comparison, VF-11 had lost as many F4Fs and almost as many pilots in just five months at Guadalcanal.

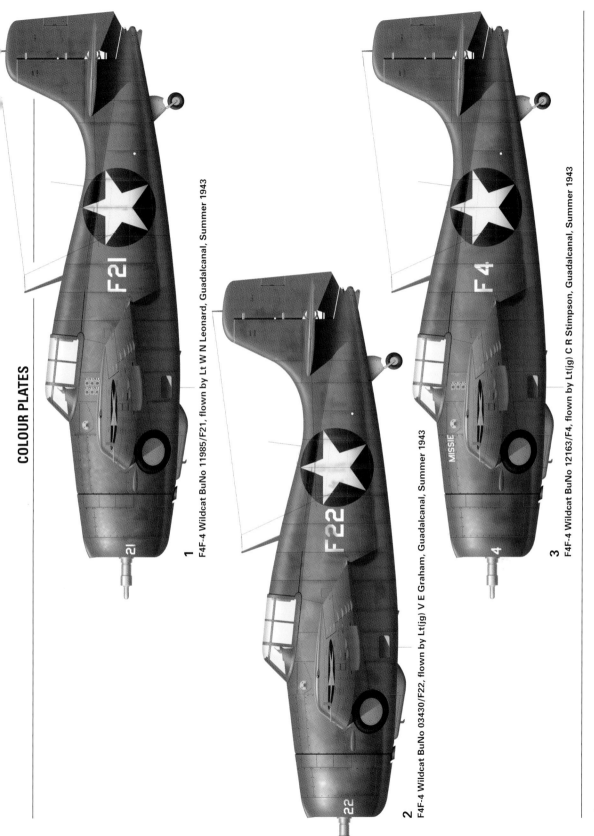

1
F4F-4 Wildcat BuNo 11985/F21, flown by Lt W N Leonard, Guadalcanal, Summer 1943

2
F4F-4 Wildcat BuNo 03430/F22, flown by Lt(jg) V E Graham, Guadalcanal, Summer 1943

3
F4F-4 Wildcat BuNo 12163/F4, flown by Lt(jg) C R Stimpson, Guadalcanal, Summer 1943

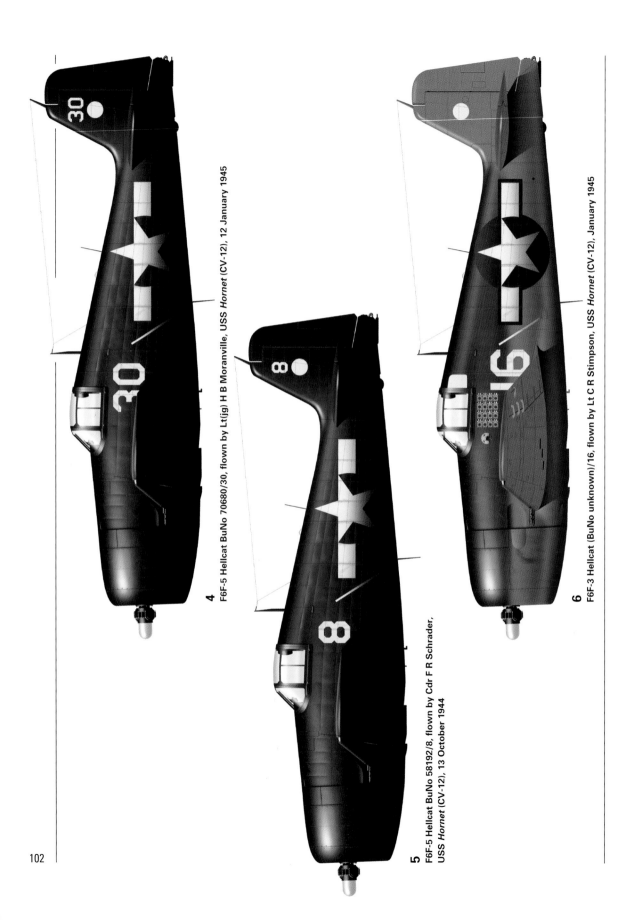

4

F6F-5 Hellcat BuNo 70680/30, flown by Lt(jg) H B Moranville, USS *Hornet* (CV-12), 12 January 1945

5

F6F-5 Hellcat BuNo 58192/8, flown by Cdr F R Schrader,
USS *Hornet* (CV-12), 13 October 1944

6

F6F-3 Hellcat (BuNo unknown)/16, flown by Lt C R Stimpson, USS *Hornet* (CV-12), January 1945

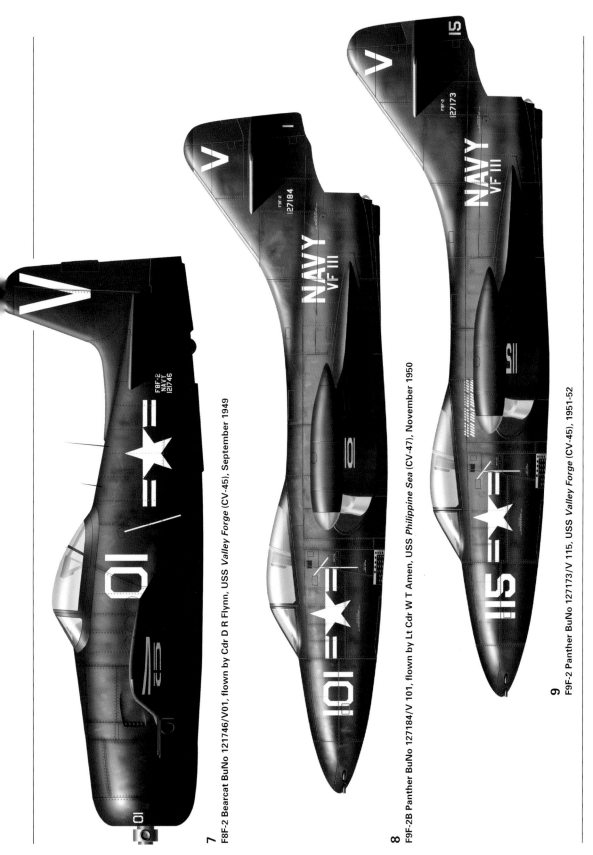

7

F8F-2 Bearcat BuNo 121746/V01, flown by Cdr D R Flynn, USS *Valley Forge* (CV-45), September 1949

8

F9F-2B Panther BuNo 127184/V 101, flown by Lt Cdr W T Amen, USS *Philippine Sea* (CV-47), November 1950

9

F9F-2 Panther BuNo 127173/V 115, USS *Valley Forge* (CV-45), 1951-52

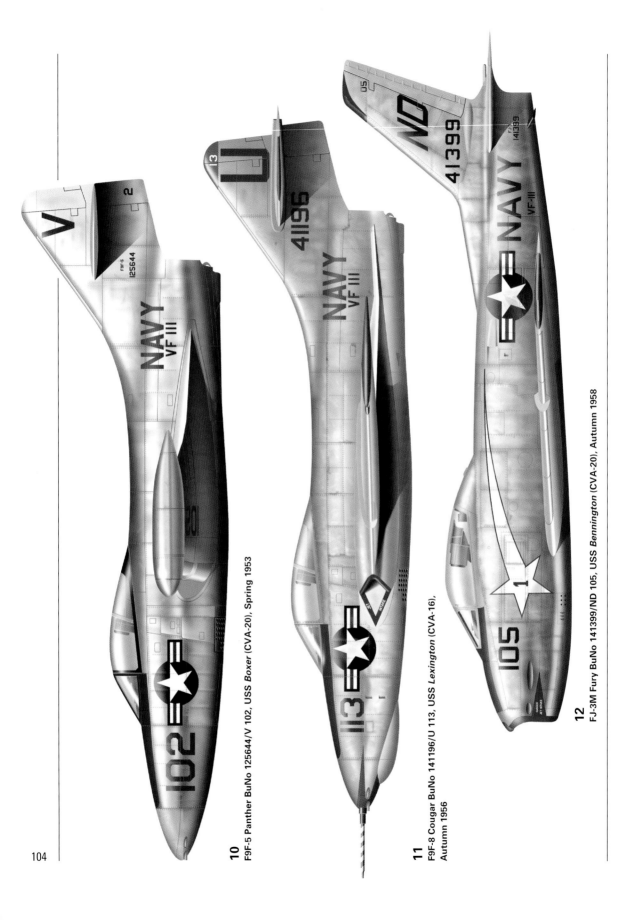

10
F9F-5 Panther BuNo 125644/V 102, USS *Boxer* (CVA-20), Spring 1953

11
F9F-8 Cougar BuNo 141196/U 113, USS *Lexington* (CVA-16),
Autumn 1956

12
FJ-3M Fury BuNo 141399/ND 105, USS *Bennington* (CVA-20), Autumn 1958

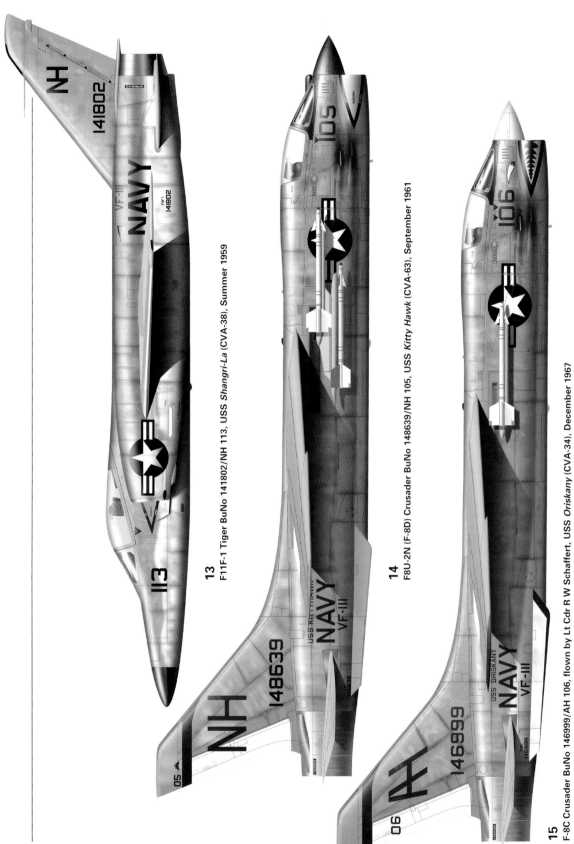

13
F11F-1 Tiger BuNo 141802/NH 113, USS *Shangri-La* (CVA-38), Summer 1959

14
F8U-2N (F-8D) Crusader BuNo 148639/NH 105, USS *Kitty Hawk* (CVA-63), September 1961

15
F-8C Crusader BuNo 146999/AH 106, flown by Lt Cdr R W Schaffert, USS *Oriskany* (CVA-34), December 1967

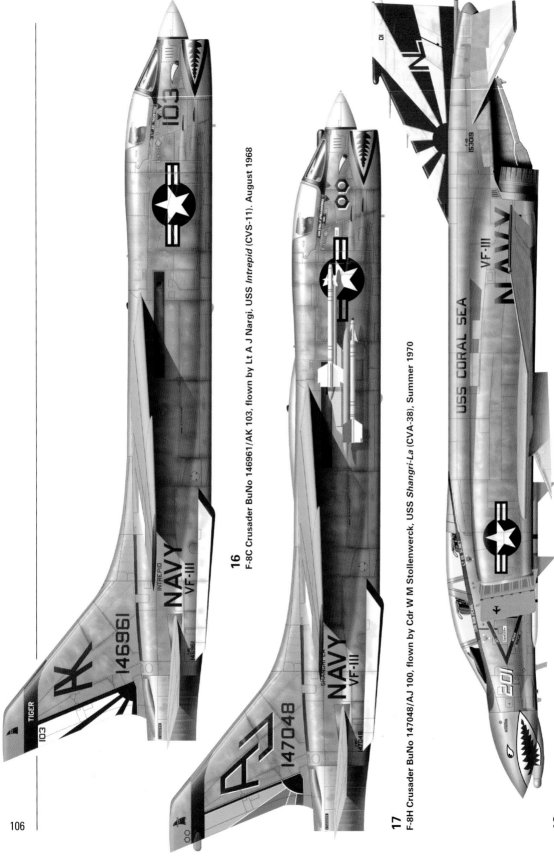

16
F-8C Crusader BuNo 146961/AK 103, flown by Lt A J Nargi, USS *Intrepid* (CVS-11), August 1968

17
F-8H Crusader BuNo 147048/AJ 100, flown by Cdr W M Stollenwerck, USS *Shangri-La* (CVA-38), Summer 1970

18
F-4B Phantom II BuNo 153019/NL 201, flown by Lt Garry Weigand and Lt(jg) Bill Freckleton, USS *Coral Sea* (CVA-43), 6 March 1972

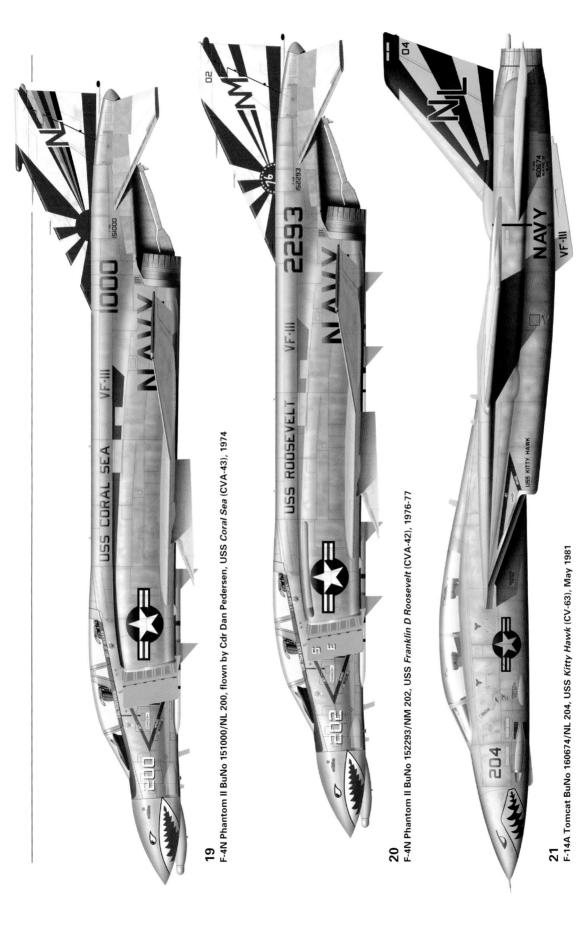

19
F-4N Phantom II BuNo 151000/NL 200, flown by Cdr Dan Pedersen, USS *Coral Sea* (CVA-43), 1974

20
F-4N Phantom II BuNo 152293/NM 202, USS *Franklin D Roosevelt* (CVA-42), 1976-77

21
F-14A Tomcat BuNo 160674/NL 204, USS *Kitty Hawk* (CV-63), May 1981

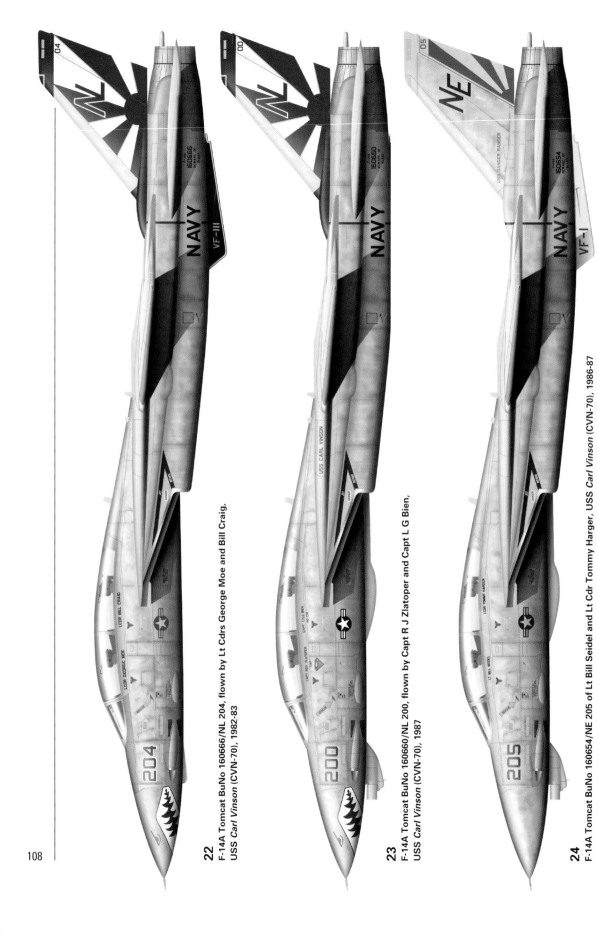

22
F-14A Tomcat BuNo 160666/NL 204, flown by Lt Cdrs George Moe and Bill Craig,
USS *Carl Vinson* (CVN-70), 1982-83

23
F-14A Tomcat BuNo 160660/NL 200, flown by Capt R J Zlatoper and Capt L G Bien,
USS *Carl Vinson* (CVN-70), 1987

24
F-14A Tomcat BuNo 160654/NE 205 of Lt Bill Seidel and Lt Cdr Tommy Harger, USS *Carl Vinson* (CVN-70), 1986-87

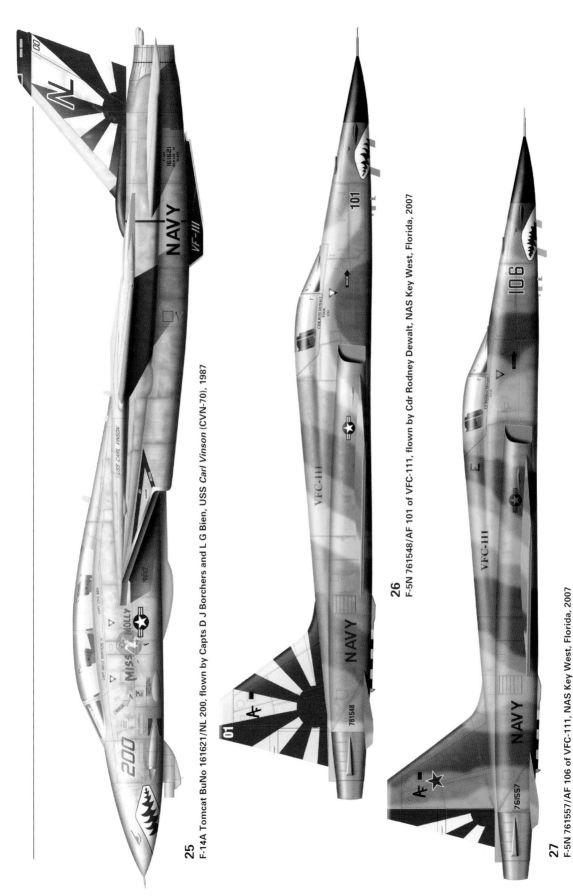

25
F-14A Tomcat BuNo 161621/NL 200, flown by Capts D J Borchers and L G Bien, USS *Carl Vinson* (CVN-70), 1987

26
F-5N 761548/AF 101 of VFC-111, flown by Cdr Rodney Dewalt, NAS Key West, Florida, 2007

27
F-5N 761557/AF 106 of VFC-111, NAS Key West, Florida, 2007

Badge 1

Badge 2

POST-VIETNAM ERA

I n the post-Vietnam doldrums, naval aviation faced a period of readjustment. In contrast to the high operating tempo from 1965 onward, carrier air wings now had ample time between deployments. For instance, *Coral Sea* had logged six combat cruises between 1964 and 1972, frequently with just five months between returning and departing. In contrast, for the rest of its career through to 1989, the carrier enjoyed 13- to 19-month intervals between deployments.

Nevertheless, commitments still had to be met. *Coral Sea* returned to WestPac in 1973 – officially a Vietnam cruise, but by then American involvement had largely ended. The 1975 deployment overlapped the communist conquest of South Vietnam, although the squadron's only 'combat' sorties were CAPs. By then VF-111 had converted to F-4Ns, which were upgraded B-models that featured enhanced avionics such as the AN/ALQ-126 electronic countermeasures package and VTAS helmet-mounted sight. Contrary to some sources, the squadron never deployed with F-4Js.

Subsequently, CVW-15 was allotted to an East Coast carrier for 1976-77, allowing the 'Sundowners' to make their first European cruise since 1948. The Sixth Fleet deployment in USS *Franklin D Roosevelt* (CV-42) became the vessel's 23rd, and final voyage, all to 'the Med'. By then the carrier was on its last legs, its poor condition being

A perennial CAG bird, BuNo 152986 went to VF-111 in 1973-74, then became VF-301's first aircraft (ND 100) in October 1975. Subsequently it flew with VMFA-321 (MG 100) circa 1977-83, and VMFA-531 (NK 200) in 1980. As an F-4N it was stricken in 1984 and placed on display in Patterson, Louisiana, in 1995 (*via Tailhook Association*)

This jet appears to be an F-4B but in fact it is an early N-model. Although the N upgrades usually involved the distinctive AN/ALQ-126 antenna behind the inlet, some were identified by the VTAS helmet sight boxes on the front canopy (*via Tailhook Association*)

BuNo 152977's traditional 'Sundowner' red-white sunburst markings with a blue stripe added to honour the US bicentennial in 1976. This jet had flown with VMFA-323 'Death Rattlers' in 1971 and, after VF-111, returned to the Marine Corps with VMFA-314 circa 1980. It was damaged beyond repair in 1983 (*via Tailhook Association*)

uncharitably described by sailors who quipped 'FDR' stood for 'filthy, dirty, rusty'.

Upon returning from cruise in April 1977, VF-111 began turning over its Phantom IIs in preparation for the newest tailhook fighter, Grumman's F-14A Tomcat. Aircrews retained through the transition period attended classes at VF-124, the Tomcat replacement squadron, while maintenance personnel were sent to the Naval Air Maintenance Training Group detachment at NAS Miramar. To fill out the squadron roster, newly minted aircrews and maintainers with no F-4 experience began checking in too.

VF-111 was fully equipped with F-14As in October 1978, and the unit flew 'turkeys' until stand-down 16 years later. It was by far the

Transition to the F-14 was noted with the creation of a 'Sundowners' Tomcat patch, which was worn by all Naval Aviators assigned to the unit. VF-111 was fully equipped with F-14As by late 1978 (*via Tailhook Association*)

The Tomcat's primary weapon was the AIM-54 Phoenix radar-guided missile, which was intended for long-range interception of enemy bombers threatening a carrier battle group. The F-14's AWG-9 onboard radar system could track and engage six targets simultaneously (*via Tailhook Association*)

'Old Nick 205' tanks during *Carl Vinson* Bering Sea operations between August 1986 and February 1987. CVW-15 Tomcats carried a variety of markings during this period in an attempt to spoof Soviet aircraft and trawlers that were monitoring their operations. These markings included the application of different tail codes, as seen here. In a subtle joke, BuNo 160654 also carried the ship name *DANGER RANGER* on its fins, although *Ranger* had actually returned from deployment in October (*via Henk van der Lugt*)

113

longest tenure of any 'Sundowner' aircraft, far exceeding the Crusader's nine-and-a-half years. From start to finish the squadron flew Grummans for 30 of its 53 years.

In 1979-80 VF-111 returned to familiar surroundings, flying from *Kitty Hawk* for the first time since 1964. In April 1980 CV-63 supported the doomed attempt to rescue US hostages in Tehran. Ironically, the operation had the potential for a Tomcat-versus-Tomcat engagement against the Islamic Republic of Iran Air Force.

There was no combat but one loss occurred. Off the Philippines on 8 September 1979, Lt Lloyd A Vermillion and Lt(jg) Richard W Cummings had barely cleared the catapult when 'Old Nick 203' suffered an engine fire. The crew had no choice but to eject from BuNo 160672, which became the first of seven VF-111 Tomcats lost from 1979 to 1992, although no aircrew perished.

Meanwhile, new carriers joined the fleet. In 1983 the 'Sundowners' completed a world tour embarked in USS *Carl Vinson* (CVN-70) as the vessel undertook its maiden deployment. It was the first of six consecutive cruises aboard 'Chuckie V'. During 1986-87 Bering Sea operations VF-111 and VF-51 spoofed the Soviets by carrying a variety of bogus tail codes. Additionally, at least one 'Sundowners' Tomcat bore the carrier name USS *Danger Ranger*!

Skipper Ray Rose (1988-89) recalls that VF-111's relationship with VF-51 in *Carl Vinson* was always good, frequently cordial. That was not always the case, as serious rivalries arose in some air wings. CVW-15's sister-squadrons exchanged parts with one another as needed, and prided themselves in flying off all 12 aircraft at the end of cruise. However, frequently in those days two jets spent most of a deployment in the hangar deck, serving as 'parts kits'.

By 1990 the F-14A, powered by Pratt & Whitney TF30s, had been in service for 15 years. Originally intended as an interim variant until aircraft fitted with General Electric F110 engines reached the fleet, the A-model became the 'any day now' Tomcat since aircrews joked 'We'll get the new aeroplane any day now'. Consequently, funding for the A-model continued to lag, and some squadrons began acquiring parts 'off the books'. In at least one instance a CO stashed Tomcat spares in his garage, away from prying eyes of officialdom.

Although the F-14's forte was fleet defence, it was versatile enough to accept other missions as well. That included reconnaissance, especially following retirement of the RA-5 Vigilante and RF-8 Crusader. Therefore, each air wing had one F-14 squadron dedicated to that role. Fitted with the Tactical Airborne Reconnaissance Pod System (TARPS), Tomcats could perform photographic and thermal 'recce' missions.

In the summer of 1982 former RF-8 pilot John Jinks was new in VF-111, but with his reconnaissance background he became the 'Sundowners'' lead TARPS pilot. Teamed with Lt(jg) Mike 'Padre' Mulcahy, Jinks represented the squadron in the annual meet at NAS Fallon, Nevada, skirting the low clouds amid snowcapped mountains. Jinks' experience in Crusaders served him well, as he was comfortable with visual navigation and took fourth place overall, first among the Tomcat squadrons.

The 'Sundowners' CAG bird intercepts a Tu-95 'Bear' during *Carl Vinson's* 1986-87 deployment that included Bering Sea operations. Shadowing the pair is an EA-6B from VAQ-134, also assigned to CVW-15. The Tomcat's canopy rails bear the names of Capts Ron 'Zap' Zlatoper and Lyle 'Ho Chi' Bien, senior CAG and deputy CAG of CVW-15 (*via Henk van der Lugt*)

With retirement of the photo-Crusader in 1987, Tomcats became carrier aviation's foremost reconnaissance platform. Led by Cdr Thomas L Mackenzie, VF-111 mastered the 'Peeping Tom' system by winning the 1990 ComAirPac TARPS derby.

In 1991 the Sundowners rode *Kitty Hawk* around the horn to return it from an East Coast update. One of the notable squadron members was AE3 Jason Lowrey in the electronics shop. He was one of two enlisted men who were 'turn qualified' to start and run the F-14s' engines. After leaving the US Navy in 1993 he pursued a career in commercial aviation and became a Boeing 777 captain with Emirates Airlines in Dubai. In retrospect he says, 'There was never a squadron like the "Sundowners"!'

At the same time CVW-15 was slated to receive F-14Ds, but *Kitty Hawk* was not yet equipped to operate the new Tomcats – a factor that boded ill for VF-111. Ultimately, 86 new or upgraded F-14B and 55 D-models were acquired, but VF-111 retained the F-14A until the 'Sundowner Sunset' in 1995.

In February 1992 Cdr Robert H Clement took over VF-111. He was an exceptionally experienced aviator, having flown in four fleet squadrons, plus an adversary unit. 'Bunga' Clement led the 'Sundowners' during the 1992-93 cruise, including sorties supporting Operations *Provide Relief* in Somalia and *Southern Watch* over Iraq. *Kitty Hawk* and CVW-15 departed San Diego in June 1994, led by

Right
'Old Nick 200' (BuNo 162594) taxies out at Fallon during CVW-15 work-ups in late 1990. Note the 25-lb practice bombs on the centreline racks (*Cdr Tom Twomey*)

Below and bottom
BuNo 162594 joined VF-111 from VF-124 in 1988 and remained with the unit through to September 1992. It later served with VF-21 and VF-154 in Japan, before returning to NAS Oceana, Virginia, in 1998 for assignment to VF-101. The jet was lost when it plunged into the Gulf of Mexico on 3 October 2002 while still with the F-14 fleet replacement squadron (*Cdr Tom Twomey*)

Above
Assigned to CVW-15 CAG Capt Rick Ludwig, BuNo 162594 featured 'Recce Rally' and 'Boola Boola' missile shoot stencils on its forward fuselage when this photograph was taken during VF-111's 1991 WestPac aboard *Kitty Hawk* (*Cdr T Twomey*)

Left
VF-111's final CAG bird is seen here ready to launch from CV-63 in 1994 (*via Henk van der Lugt*)

The 'Sundowners' Sunset' was commemorated with this patch (*via Tailhook Association*)

Cdr Donnie L Cochran, a former *Blue Angel*. Originally intended for a Persian Gulf cruise, the battle group was diverted to Korean waters on yet another 'show the flag' mission so typical of carrier deployments. Tensions in the region led to the decision to place the battle group in the Yellow Sea and Sea of Japan. An airborne change of command occurred on 1 September as Cdr Cochran turned over to his executive officer, Cdr Thomas M Joyce, a Naval Flight Officer (RIO). The

117

'ceremony' occurred at *700 mph*, 500 ft overhead *Kitty Hawk*. After a low pass, Cochran lit his afterburners and climbed vertically through the cloud deck.

The balance of the 1994 deployment involved some potential excitement, as reportedly VF-111 encountered 'Chinese' jets that were actually North Korean. 'The Hawk' returned to San Diego just before Christmas, and 'Croc' Joyce would prove to be the 'Sundowners'' last commanding officer.

With the end of the Cold War, force structure was bound to be pared as President Bill Clinton and the Republican-controlled congress were eager to grasp the perceived 'peace dividend'. Although the benefit proved illusory, historic squadrons were chopped nevertheless. They included VA-35 'Black Panthers', which traced its heritage to 1934, and whose Dauntlesses had sunk three Japanese carriers in World War 2. But just as the bureaucrats ended the life of the US Navy's oldest attack squadron, they also slew VF-111 along with the rest of CVW-15 (bar VFA-27, VFA-97 and HS-4). For the 'Sundowners', WestPac 94 was 'the last sunset', and for the 'Screaming Eagles' of VF-51, it was 'the last scream'.

Both VF-111 and VF-51 were deserving of preservation, as no other US Navy squadrons had scored aerial kills in three wars. Meanwhile, some relatively new F/A-18 squadrons were preserved, while the surviving Tomcat units transitioned to Super Hornets the following decade.

The formal disestablishment was held at NAS Miramar on 16 February 1995, with all personnel and equipment transferred by the end of March. When the 'Sundowner Sunset' event was held that month, VF-111 observed 36 years of continuous service since the VA-156 takeover in 1959. But the 'Sundowner' tradition and heritage extended back 53 years, to the era when decks were straight and wooden, when Grummans had tailwheels and Pratt & Whitneys swung propellers.

After VJ-Day, the 'Sundowners'' first skipper, Cdr Clarence M White, reflected, 'Fighting the peace is not half as much fun as fighting the war. The chaos is so much more disorganised'. A legion of 'Sundowners' from 1942 to 1995 doubtless would exclaim, 'Bravo Zulu, Skipper!'

AFTER THE SUNSET

In 1988 the 'Sundowners' held the first of 15 annual reunions, organised by Kermit and Violet Enander. 'Tim' had received his nickname while Charlie Stimpson's plane captain in 1943, and continued in aviation. In 1946 he was hired as a United Airlines mechanic and rose to master sergeant in the Marine Corps Reserve, serving during the Korean War. Subsequently Enander earned a master's degree and was a teacher for 25 years. The first event was a huge success with 160 former squadron members attending.

As the VF-11/111 reunions prospered, 'Bombing' and 'Torpedo 11' were brought into the fold as 'The Sun Downers and Carrier Air Group 11 Association', incorporated in Washington State. Eventually the Enanders had 250 pilot and aircrew names on the roster. The final air group reunion was held in 2002, seven years after VF-111's stand-down.

'Vi' Enander died in 2008 after 62 years of marriage, and Tim returned to his roots. Today he says, 'I am just an old former "Sundowner" living in my home town of Roseburg, Oregon'. No one has done as much to perpetrate the squadron's continuing legacy.

The 'Sundowners' name lay dormant for more than a decade, and though the genealogy was forever severed, the legacy was revived. In 2006 the US Navy Reserve's VFC-13 'Fighting Saints' (a fleet adversary squadron), based at NAS Fallon, maintained a detachment at NAS Key West, Florida. Because Key West supports the Strike Fighter Air Combat Readiness Program, a larger capability was required. Therefore, a permanent, full-sized unit was authorised, but identity of the new squadron was yet undetermined.

Enter 'Sundowners' historian Henk van der Lugt. At the 2006 Tailhook Association reunion he approached the commander and deputy commander of Carrier Reserve Air Wing 20, which controlled adversary units, suggesting the 'Sundowner' name. Henk was in good company, as the CO of VFC-13 was Cdr James 'Guido' DeMatteo, whose father had flown in VF-111. Consequently, that November the Key West 'det' became VFC-111 under Cdr Rodney DeWalt. Flying 12 Northrop F-5N Tiger IIs, the 'Sundowners' provide dissimilar air-to-air combat training (DACT) for all US Navy and Marine Corps F/A-18 fleet replacement squadrons. The four 'client' units are VFA-106 (NAS Oceana, Virginia), VFA-122 and VFA-125 (NAS Lemoore, California) and VMFAT-101 (MCAS Miramar, California), which train fleet-ready strike-fighter pilots.

In 2007 a dedicated adversary squadron was established at NAS Key West. In honour of the 'Sundowners'' historic record, the new unit was designated VFC-111, flying Northrop F-5Ns. AF 101 provided a contrast in markings with the vivid sunburst tail and 'sharkmouths' superimposed on a tactical grey scheme (*José Ramos*)

Boasting a reduced sunburst marking on its rudder only, AF 106 has been camouflagd in a three-tone desert colour scheme (*José Ramos*)

Embracing the 'Sundowner' tradition, VFC-111 adopted the historic unit emblem and the call sign 'Bandit'. Although nominally a Reserve squadron, the 'Omars' actually have active Reserve and Regular US Navy personnel both in the cockpits of their jets and in support positions on the ground.

The original 'Sundowners' are long gone, but their heritage and tradition remain – testament to one of the finest records in the long history of naval aviation.

The current 'Sundowners', VFC-111, modified the traditional setting sun emblem with two F-5s in place of the World War 2 Grumman fighters (*via José Ramos*)

APPENDICES

VF-11/111 'SUNDOWNERS' AIRCRAFT

August 1942	Grumman F4F-4 Wildcat	January 1959	Grumman F11F-1 Tiger
September 1943	Grumman F6F-3/5 Hellcat	May 1961	Vought F8U-2N (F-8D) Crusader
December 1946	Grumman F8F-1 Bearcat	circa April 1966	Vought F-8E Crusader
March 1949	Grumman F8F-2 Bearcat	circa February 1967	Vought F-8C Crusader
December 1949	Grumman F9F-2 Panther	circa December 1968	Vought F-8H Crusader
September 1952	Grumman F9F-5 Panther	January 1971	McDonnell Douglas F-4B Phantom II
December 1953	Grumman F9F-6 Cougar	March 1974	McDonnell Douglas F-4N Phantom II
June 1955	Grumman F9F-8 Cougar	October 1978	Grumman F-14A Tomcat
August 1957	North American FJ-3 Fury	March 1995	Disestablished

VF-11/111 'SUNDOWNERS' DEPLOYMENTS

1943	Guadalcanal	CVG-11	F4F-4	Southwest Pacific
1944-45	Hornet	CVG-11	F6F-3/5	WestPac
1947-48	Valley Forge	CVAG-11	F8F-1	World
1950	Philippine Sea	CVG-11	F9F-2	Korea
1951-52	Valley Forge	ATG-1	F9F-2	Korea
1953	Boxer	ATG-1	F9F-5	Korea (March-November)
1953	Lake Champlain	CVG-4	F9F-5	Korea (April-December)
1956	Lexington	ATG-1	F9F-8	WestPac
1958-59	Bennington	ATG-4	FJ-3	WestPac
1959	Shangri-La	CVG-11	F11F-1	WestPac
1960-61	Hancock	CVG-11	F11F-1	WestPac
1961	Kitty Hawk	CVW-11	F8U-2N	Lant (August-November)/WestPac
1962-63	Kitty Hawk	CVG-11	F8U-2N	WestPac
1963-64	Kitty Hawk	CVW-11	F-8D	WestPac/Vietnam
1965	Midway	CVW-2	F-8D	WestPac/Vietnam
1966	Oriskany	CVW-16	F-8E	WestPac/Vietnam
1967	Oriskany	CVW-16	F-8E	WestPac/Vietnam
1967	Intrepid det	CVW-10	F-8C	WestPac/Vietnam
1968	Intrepid det	CVW-10	F-8C	WestPac/Vietnam
1969	Ticonderoga	CVW-16	F-8H	WestPac/Vietnam
1970	Shangri-La	CVW-8	F-8H	WestPac/Vietnam
1971-72	Coral Sea	CVW-15	F-4B	WestPac/Vietnam
1973	Coral Sea	CVW-15	F-4B	WestPac/Vietnam
1974-75	Coral Sea	CVW-15	F-4N	WestPac
1976-77	Franklin D Roosevelt	CVW-19	F-4N	Mediterranean
1979-80	Kitty Hawk	CVW-15	F-14A	WestPac/Indian Ocean
1981	Kitty Hawk	CVW-15	F-14A	WestPac/Indian Ocean
1983	Carl Vinson	CVW-15	F-14A	World
1984-85	Carl Vinson	CVW-15	F-14A	Pacific

1986-87	Carl Vinson	CVW-15	F-14A	NorPac/WestPac/Indian Ocean
1988	Carl Vinson	CVW-15	F-14A	NorPac/WestPac/Indian Ocean
1989	Carl Vinson	CVW-15	F-14A	NorPac/WestPac
1990	Carl Vinson	CVW-15	F-14A	WestPac/Indian Ocean
1992-93	Kitty Hawk	CVW-15	F-14A	WestPac/Indian Ocean/Persian Gulf
1994	Kitty Hawk	CVW-15	F-14A	WestPac/Indian Ocean

VF-11 'SUNDOWNERS' ACES

VF-11 Score	Score	Breakdown	Notes
Lt Charles R Stimpson	16	6 F4F, 10 F6F	Died 1983
Lt James S Swope	9.666	4.666 F4F, 5 F6F	Died 2000
Lt Jimmie E Savage	7	F6F	Died 1984
Lt(jg) H Blake Moranville	6	F6F	Died 2000
Lt Cdr Robert E Clements	5	F6F	Died 1989
Lt(jg) Vernon E Graham	5	F4F	Died 2006
Lt Henry S White	5	2 F4F, 3 F6F	Died 1972
Lt John A Zink	3	F6F plus 2 in VF-18/17	
Lt William N Leonard	2	F4F plus 4 in VF-42/3	Died 2005
Lt(jg) William E Masoner	2	F4F plus 10 in VF-19	Died 1986
Lt(jg) W Robert Maxwell	0	7 in VF-51	

VF-11/111 'SUNDOWNERS' MEMORIALS

The Pima Air Museum in Tucson, Arizona, has F-14A BuNo 160684 in its original 1978 VF-111 markings, NL 211.

The Palm Springs Air Museum, California, displays BuNo 58369 on a composite Hellcat with No 36 Hornet markings, but in an incorrect tri-colour scheme.

The F-8K aboard USS Midway (CV-41) in San Diego is dedicated to three 'Sundowners' lost during the vessel's 1965 Vietnam deployment – skippers Doyle Lynn and James La Haye, and Lt(jg) Gene Gollahan. The F-8K is painted as F-8D NE 461, with BuNo 140730. The aircraft's actual BuNo is 154370.

The Pacific Coast Aviation Museum in Santa Rosa, California, displays F-8C BuNo 146995 as AH 125.

The F-8C (BuNo 145449) displayed at the Naval Strike Air Warfare Center at NAS Fallon, Nevada, carries Dick Schaffert's name beneath its canopy.

At NAS Key West, Florida, VF-111's MiG kill F-4B is displayed on a pedestal inside the front gate. VFC-111 had the veteran Phantom II repainted to resemble its markings in 1972. The new 'Sundowners' invited Garry Weigand and Bill Freckleton to the dedication ceremony on 21 March 2008

COLOUR PLATES

1

F4F-4 Wildcat BuNo 11985/F21, flown by Lt W N Leonard, Guadalcanal, Summer 1943

'Fighting 11' was unusual in that it assigned individual aircraft to most pilots. This was partly because enough F4Fs were available to support such a scheme by early 1943. BuNo 11985 belonged to Lt William N Leonard, who was one of the US Navy's most experienced fighter pilots in the first half of 1942, having seen action in the Battles of Coral Sea (VF-42) and Midway (VF-3). With four confirmed victories from that period, Leonard began his Guadalcanal tour with the appropriate number of 'rising sun' flags applied to his aeroplane, and he added two more 'Zekes' to that score near the Russell Islands on 12 June 1943. Leonard subsequently served on the staff of TF-38 in 1944-45.

2

F4F-4 Wildcat BuNo 03430/F22, flown by Lt(jg) V E Graham, Guadalcanal, Summer 1943

'Fox 22' was the assigned aircraft of Lt(jg) Vernon E Graham, VF-11's first ace. He was designated a Naval Aviator in April 1942 and arrived with the squadron on Guadalcanal a year later. On 12 June 1943, flying BuNo 12119, he was credited with downing five A6M5 Zero-sens in a dogfight northwest of the Russell Islands. Graham's fuel was exhausted in the combat and he attempted a dead-stick landing, overshooting the Russells' runway and destroying the aeroplane (side number unknown). Although badly injured, Graham survived to receive the Navy Cross, and left the service, having fully recovered, in September 1945.

3

F4F-4 Wildcat BuNo 12163/F4, flown by Lt(jg) C R Stimpson, Guadalcanal, Summer 1943

Charles R 'Skull' Stimpson proved one of the most efficient fighter pilots in the US Navy. Commissioned in May 1942, he joined VF-11 in July and spent nearly the entire war with the unit. At Guadalcanal he flew this machine with the name *MISSIE* in white block letters ahead of the squadron emblem. Stimpson claimed six victories in three actions, including four D3A 'Vals' on 16 June 1943. His other claims were Zero-sens over Kula Gulf (on 6 July) and Rendova (on 9 July). Stimpson continued his record as the 'Sundowners'' leading scorer aboard *Hornet* in 1944-45.

4

F6F-5 Hellcat BuNo 70680/30, flown by Lt(jg) H B Moranville, USS *Hornet* (CV-12), 12 January 1945

Blake Moranville joined the 'Sundowners' as a 20-year-old ensign in 1943. Flying Hellcats during the *Hornet* deployment, he scored his first success by downing an 'Oscar' over the Philippines on 18 October 1944, adding a 'Betty' and two 'Tojos' on 5 November. Moranville became an ace at 21, claiming a 'Dinah' on 19 November and another Ki-46 on 14 December. On 12 January 1945 he was flying 'Ginger 30' when it was hit by AA near Saigon, leading to a forced landing. Moranville was held by the Vichy French until permitted to escape with other PoWs later that year. He remained in the US Navy post-war, retiring as a lieutenant commander in 1964.

5

F6F-5 Hellcat BuNo 58192/8, flown by Cdr F R Schrader, USS *Hornet* (CV-12), 13 October 1944

Cdr Frederick R Schrader was a 1935 graduate of the US Naval Academy who served the required period aboard surface ships before earning his wings in 1940. Schrader led VF-3 from October 1943 through to August 1944, when he was designated Commander Air Group 11. He was one of 42 members of his academy class who died in World War 2. It is uncertain whether Schrader had a personal 'CAG bird', as did many air group commanders, but he was definitely flying this Hellcat when he was shot down and killed while strafing a Japanese seaplane base on Formosa on 13 October 1944. Based on the side number, the fighter's usual call sign would have been 'Ginger 8', although most CAGs used the identifier '99' when aloft.

6

F6F-3 Hellcat (BuNo unknown)/16, flown by Lt C R Stimpson, USS *Hornet* (CV-12), January 1945

At the end of the *Hornet* deployment in February 1945, VF-11 pilots posed for what Charlie Stimpson called 'I love me' photos. This F6F-3, probably side number 16, was bedecked with the squadron emblem and 16 rising sun victory flags, denoting Stimpson's wartime total, including six at Guadalcanal. The distinctive 'Sundowners' logo, which had been applied to each Wildcat on Guadalcanal, was notably absent from Hellcats during the *Hornet* cruise in 1944-45. Apparently, each pilot sat in this aircraft (BuNo unknown) and the appropriate number of victory flags was added during the photographic session. About the same time Stimpson posed in F6F-5 side number 29, with the same victory tally but no squadron emblem.

7

F8F-2 Bearcat BuNo 121746/V01, flown by Cdr D R Flynn, USS *Valley Forge* (CV-45), September 1949

VF-11 became VF-11A in a US Navy-wide squadron redesignation scheme in 1946, and it was redesignated VF-111 two years later. The 'Sundowners' flew both versions of the Bearcat, receiving F8F-1s in late 1946 and taking them on the *Valley Forge's* world cruise two years later. Although the immediate post-war era was marked by declining budgets that reduced pilots' flight time, some new aeroplanes still reached the frontline. In early 1949 'Fighting 111' converted to 'dash two' Bearcats, mostly armed with four 20 mm cannon. Both models bore similar markings, with the *Valley Forge* air group V symbol on the tail and side numbers in the 100 series.

8

F9F-2B Panther BuNo 127184/V 101, flown by Lt Cdr W T Amen, USS *Philippine Sea* (CV-47), November 1950

V 101 was the Panther assigned to Lt Cdr William T Amen, commanding officer of VF-111 during the squadron's initial Korean War deployment in *Philippine Sea*. Flying a VF-112 aeroplane, Amen shot down a Soviet MiG-15 during strikes against the Yalu River bridges on 9 November – the first verified jet-to-jet aerial victory in history. Previously, that honour was thought to belong to 1Lt Russell Brown, a USAF F-80 pilot who had claimed a MiG kill the day before – his foe safely made it back to base, however. Owing to maintenance requirements, it was not unusual for two F9F squadrons on the same ship to fly one another's aircraft interchangeably.

9

F9F-2 Panther BuNo 127173/V 115, USS *Valley Forge* (CV-45), 1951-52

During their second Korean War cruise the 'Sundowners' continued flying F9F-2s, assigned to their pre-war carrier, *Valley Forge,* from October 1951 to July 1952. Transferred in from CAG-11, VF-111 was assigned to the makeshift ATG-1, joining squadrons from three other air groups to meet the pressing needs of additional carriers off Korea. ATG-1 included VF-52's F9F-2s, VF-653's F4U-4 Corsairs and VA-194's AD-2/3 Skyraiders. This VF-111 Panther sports some 40 mission markers, each sortie denoted by a white bomb. Unlike the 1950 cruise in *Philippine Sea*, subsequent deployments involved no MiG engagements, so the jet fighters concentrated on strike, defence suppression and combat air patrols.

10

F9F-5 Panther BuNo 125644/V 102, USS *Boxer* (CVA-20) Spring 1953

VF-111's third, and final, Korean War deployment began on board *Boxer* in March 1953, again as part of ATG-1. Each squadron in the group retained its parent carrier's markings, hence the V tail code on VF-111's bare metal aircraft. However, operating new F9F-5s with *Boxer's* old-style catapults posed serious operational problems in respect to launch weights and ordnance loads. Consequently, in June ATG-1 'cross-decked' VF-111 and its new Panthers to *Lake Champlain* in exchange for a CAG-4 Corsair squadron. On 27 July a 'Sundowner' division claimed the distinction of dropping the US Navy's last bombs of the Korean War.

11

F9F-8 Cougar BuNo 141196/U 113, USS *Lexington* (CVA-16), Autumn 1956

The VF-111's only deployment in the swept-wing Grumman Cougar was with ATG-1 aboard *Lexington* in the second half of 1956. In contrast to the previous overall dark blue, from 1955 US Navy aircraft switched to a colour scheme of matt gull grey uppersurfaces over insignia white undersides. This cruise was VF-111's third consecutive deployment with an ATG rather than a conventional air group. Contrary to usual air task group markings, each squadron displayed the ATG-1 'U' tail code rather than retaining the original identifying letter. Other squadrons within ATG-1 in 1956 included VF-52 with F2H-3 Banshees, VA-151 with F7U-3 Cutlasses and VA-196 with AD-6 Skyraiders.

12

FJ-3M Fury BuNo 141399/ND 105, USS *Bennington* (CVA-20), Autumn 1958

VF-111 flew the North American Fury during 1957-58, being one of the later squadrons to receive the type. The FJ-3 entered fleet service in May 1955, with the -3M version being capable of carrying the AIM-9 Sidewinder air-to-air missile. The 'dash three' was also fitted with a probe-and-drogue in-flight refuelling capability. Assigned

to ATG-4, the squadron cruised aboard *Bennington* from August 1958 to January 1959 – the 'Sundowners'' fourth, and last, deployment with an ATG. The squadron's Furies often sported a white star with a red outline and the number '1' in the middle, signifying the squadron's previous association with ATG-1.

13

F11F-1 Tiger BuNo 141802/NH 113, USS *Shangri-La* (CVA-38), Summer 1959

Only seven squadrons flew the Grumman Tiger, which deployed in five carriers. The type served for just four years with the fleet before being replaced by the far more capable Vought F8U Crusader. The 'Sundowners' operated the F11F for two-and-a-half years, deploying to the Western Pacific with CAG-11 aboard *Shangri-La* in 1959. It was VF-111's first cruise with its parent air group in nine years, followed by a CVG-11 deployment aboard *Hancock* in 1960-61. BuNo 141802 also served with VF-191 and, wearing generic Marine Corps markings, was displayed at New Bern, North Carolina, as recently as 2006.

14

F8U-2N (F-8D) Crusader BuNo 148639/NH 105, USS *Kitty Hawk* (CVA-63), September 1961

VF-111 received its first Vought Crusaders in April 1961 and flew them until transitioning to F-4B Phantom IIs nine years later. This aircraft was one of the 'Sundowners'' early F8U-2Ns, which was engaged in initial carrier qualifications aboard *Kitty Hawk* in September 1961. Note the dark coloured 'Omar' emblem ahead of the '05' numeral on the jet's vertical fin. The 'Omar' mascot marked VF-111's transition to supersonic aircraft, and it remained for the duration of the squadron's existence. The F8U-2N's designation was altered to F-8D in the tri-service change that also took place in September 1961. Subsequently upgraded to F-8H specification, this aeroplane was written off in a non-fatal accident while serving with Test and Evaluation Squadron VX-4 on 20 April 1970.

15

F-8C Crusader BuNo 146999/AH 106, flown by Lt Cdr R W Schaffert, USS *Oriskany* (CVA-34), December 1967

Lt Cdr Richard 'Brown Bear' Schaffert flew 'Old Nick 106' in his epic solo combat against four MiG-17s while escorting an A-4 Skyhawk on 14 December 1967. The action was vividly depicted by computer graphics on The History Channel television program *Dogfights* in 2007. Schaffert's assigned aircraft was '103', as side numbers were allotted in order of pilot seniority. Therefore, AH 106 probably bore the name of Lt Cdr Bob Jurgens. Schaffert flew BuNo 146999 on five missions during the deployment, and saw MiGs on three of them! This aircraft is honoured at NAS Fallon, Nevada, home of the US Navy's Strike Air Warfare Center.

16

F-8C Crusader BuNo 146961/AK 103, flown by Lt A J Nargi, USS *Intrepid* (CVS-11), August 1968

The 'Sundowners' provided fighter detachments to the antisubmarine carrier *Intrepid* on two cruises – May to December 1967 and June 1968 to February 1969. The 1967 'modex' markings were AH XX, and in 1968-69 AK 1XX.

'Old Nick 103' was flown by Lt Anthony J Nargi when he shot down a MiG-21 on 1 August 1968. The name *TIGER* on the tail stripe was the call sign of the assigned pilot, Lt Joe Thompson. Modified to F-8K status, BuNo 146961 was released by the US Navy and eventually obtained by Energetic Materials Research and Testing Centre at Socorro, New Mexico. Internet evidence shows that it remained there in 2004.

17

F-8H Crusader BuNo 147048/AJ 100, flown by Cdr W M Stollenwerck, USS *Shangri-La* (CVA-38), Summer 1970

'Double nuts' was VF-111's 'CAG bird' aboard *Shangri-La* for the 1970 deployment with CVW-8. The rudder displayed the colours of each squadron – red, green, blue, yellow and rust brown. Lasting from March to December, it was the squadron's longest cruise of the Vietnam War. However, that year marked a low point in naval aviation activity during the conflict, with few losses in Southeast Asia. Cdr Stollenwerck departed the ship mid-cruise, being briefly succeeded by Cdr C G Dimon in June. In turn Dimon was relieved by his executive officer, Cdr Bill Rennie. BuNo 147048 was written off in a 'stateside' accident while serving with US Marine Corps Reserve unit VMFA-112 in May 1973.

18

F-4B Phantom II BuNo 153019/NL 201, flown by Lt Garry Weigand and Lt(jg) Bill Freckleton, USS *Coral Sea* (CVA-43), 6 March 1972

During *Coral Sea's* 1971-72 cruise, NL 201 'belonged' to the squadron CO – the names carried on the canopies were *CDR BOB PEARL* and *LT GIL SLINEY*. Delivered in 1966, BuNo 153019 flew with VF-213 from *Kitty Hawk* during three Vietnam cruises, downing an An-2 on 20 December 1966. The jet was then transferred to VF-121 at NAS Miramar, where it served from 1969-71, prior to joining VF-111 when the unit replaced its Crusaders with Phantom IIs. After two 'Sundowners' deployments and an upgrade to F-4N specification, BuNo 153019 served with VMFA-531 at MCAS El Toro, California, in 1974-75, then reserve-manned VF-201 at NAF Dallas, Texas, in 1977-84, before ending its flying days with VF-171 at NAS Key West, Florida. Repainted as 'Old Nick 201', the jet was dedicated as the 'gate guard' at NAS Key West in 2008.

19

F-4N Phantom II BuNo 151000/NL 200, flown by Cdr Dan Pedersen, USS *Coral Sea* (CVA-43), 1974

Another 'CAG bird', NL 200 displayed five vari-coloured stripes on the tail representing each squadron in CVW-15. The 'Sundowners'' third *Coral Sea* deployment lasted from December 1974 to July 1975, coinciding with South Vietnam's collapse. Nearly 230 F-4Bs received upgrades to N-model status in the 'Bee Line' programme to extend airframe fatigue life. While retaining many F-4B features, the N-models boasted aerodynamic improvements and the AN/ALQ-126 electronic countermeasure suite. Some aircraft were also modified to allow the crew to wear helmet-mounted sights. The 'Sundowners' began receiving F-4Ns in April 1974, when Cdr W E Markley was the unit CO. The rear canopy rail of this jet bore the name of AE1 J C Decker, who was almost certainly VF-111's 'sailor of the year'.

20

F-4N Phantom II BuNo 152293/NM 202, USS *Franklin D Roosevelt* (CVA-42), 1976-77

Sporting US Bicentennial markings, VF-111 aircraft replaced a red sunray with a red/white/blue one in the traditional anniversary colours in 1976. Additionally, the splitter vane of this jet features the safety 'S' and battle efficiency 'E', which denotes that VF-111 was the best unit in those categories among all Naval Air Forces Pacific fighter squadrons for that year. The *Roosevelt* cruise with CVW-19 was the 'Sundowners'' fourth, and last, in Phantom IIs, and their only dedicated Mediterranean deployment, although the squadron had passed through 'the Med' embarked in *Valley Forge* in 1948, and it would also do so during *Carl Vinson's* maiden voyage in 1983. For the 1976-77 'FDR' cruise, VF-111 and VF-51 replaced VF-191 and VF-194, which were busy converting from Crusaders to Phantom IIs.

21

F-14A Tomcat BuNo 160674/NL 204, USS *Kitty Hawk* (CV-63), May 1981

The US Navy's previous glossy grey and white colour scheme was replaced in 1978 with a matt-finish overall light gull grey (FS 16440) that reduced glare, before the tactical paint scheme (TPS) was fully adopted in the early 1980s. Of necessity the 16640 scheme forced a notable change upon the 'Sundowners'' typical bright colours. Nonetheless, the squadron retained the sunburst emblem in black rather than red and white. This change was also forced upon the traditional 'sharksmouth' on the radome too. *USS KITTY HAWK* was stencilled along the outer edge of the engine inlet, but no aircrew names were carried on this particular jet. VF-111 deployed in these colours from April to November 1981 in the familiar waters of the Western Pacific and Indian Ocean. Issued new to VF-111 in late 1978, this aircraft was lost during the deployment when the crew was forced to eject on 27 June 1981 while in the landing pattern after a mission over the Arabian Sea. Both fliers reported smoke in the cockpit, erratic control inputs and control panel warning lights. The RIO initiated a command ejection and the crew was recovered with minor injuries.

22

F-14A Tomcat BuNo 160666/NL 204, flown by Lt Cdrs George Moe and Bill Craig, USS *Carl Vinson* (CVN-70), 1982-83

When F-14s entered service in 1974 the paint scheme was light gull grey with white undersurfaces. As mentioned in the previous plates commentary, in 1978 the 'Sundowners'' first F-14A Tomcats arrived directly from Grumman in overall light gull grey, minus the full nose and tail markings previously carried on the unit's F-8 Crusaders and F-4 Phantom IIs. During a prolonged period ashore between the 1981 and 1982/83 cruises, the CO, Cdr Stuart O Schmitt, and his maintenance officer decided to revert to the full sunrays on the tail, red modex numbers with white outlines and a full colour 'sharksmouth', versus the more conventional black or white counter-shaded variety. These markings were borne during the squadron's first cruise in *Carl Vinson*, which took the unit around the world from March to October 1983. Issued new to VF-111 in June 1978, this jet later became the 'CAG bird' in the mid-1980s, before being transferred to VF-21 in 1989. It was passed on to the Pacific Missile Test Center at NAS Point Mugu, California, two years later. Retired in the late 1990s, BuNo 160666 presently resides in the Western Aerospace Museum in Oakland, California.

23

F-14A Tomcat BuNo 160660/NL 200, flown by Capt R J Zlatoper and Capt L G Bien, USS *Carl Vinson* (CVN-70), 1987

This Tomcat carried the names of Capts Ronald J Zlatoper and Lyle G Bien during *Carl Vinson's* Western Pacific and Indian Ocean deployment that ran from August 1986 to February 1987. The Superman logo below the pilot's cockpit was applied in honour of Capt Zlatoper's status of 'Super CAG', as the senior air wing commander was called at that time. Additionally, the call signs *"ZAP"* and *HO CHI* were painted below their respective names. Zlatoper, originally an A-6 Intruder pilot, attained the rank of full admiral and commanded the US Pacific Fleet in 1994-96. Bien, an NFO, retired as a vice admiral in 1998. This aircraft was painted overall satin light gull grey FS 26440. Originally delivered new to VF-124 in April 1978, BuNo 160660 was transferred to VF-111 in 1982. After three deployments with the unit, the aircraft was passed on to newly commissioned VF-194 in January 1988, although it had joined VF-51 before year-end after the unit was cut with the disbanding of CVW-10. BuNo 160660 was written off while still serving with the unit when, on 16 July 1991, the fighter crashed into the Straits of Formosa, off Northwest Africa, when the arrestor cable broke on landing aboard USS *Ranger* (CV-61). Both crewmen successfully ejected.

24

F-14A Tomcat BuNo 160654/NE 205 of Lt Bill Seidel and Lt Cdr Tommy Harger, USS *Carl Vinson* (CVN-70), 1986-87

During *Carl Vinson's* North Pacific cruise in 1986-87, VF-111 and VF-51 carried CVW-2 markings to deceive Soviet spy vessels and reconnaissance aircraft that were shadowing the carrier. 'Sundown 205' displays the *Ranger* NE tailcode and the titling *USS DANGER RANGER* on its fin – *Ranger* had returned from its most recent deployment in October 1986, two months after CVN-70 had deployed. The deception also included *VF-1* being sprayed onto the fuselage strake. The 1986-87 cruise marked the first time that a carrier had operated north of the Aleutians in many years, well within range of Soviet land-based aircraft and contrary to the usual mid-Pacific 'Bear box'. The overall colour scheme of this aircraft was gull grey FS 16440. RIO Harger had previously flown Phantom IIs with VF-111 in the 1970s. Delivered to VF-124 in January 1978, this aircraft was assigned to VF-111 on two separate occasions from December 1981 to August 1986 and from January 1988 to December 1992. It also served with VF-2 and VF-101. Stricken in April 1995, it was scrapped at NAS Oceana several years later.

25

F-14A Tomcat BuNo 161621/NL 200, flown by Capts D J Borchers and L G Bien, USS *Carl Vinson* (CVN-70), 1987

This aircraft was unusual in that it boasted prominent nose art, which usually was officially discouraged – especially since pin-ups were considered politically incorrect.

However, the art was chosen as a tribute to Molly Sneed, who had christened CVN-70 in 1980 at Senator Carl Vinson's request, as she and her husband had been his longtime aides. *MISS MOLLY* titling had previously adorned CVW-15's C-1A COD in the early 1980s. Capt Borchers was *Carl Vinson's* executive officer in 1984 and its captain from 1989 to 1992. Delivered new to VF-21 in February 1984, BuNo 161621 served with VF-111, VF-213, VF-124 and VF-154, prior to being stricken in 2004.

26

F-5N 761548/AF 101 of VFC-111, flown by Cdr Rodney Dewalt, NAS Key West, Florida, 2007

In 2006 the Navy established a new adversary squadron, VFC-111, at NAS Key West, Florida. Expanded from the original VFC-13 detachment flying the Northrop F-5N Tiger II, the new 'Sundowners' provide air-to-air training for US Navy and Marine Corps fleet replacement squadrons, as well as Regular and Reserve USAF units and the Air National Guard. The brilliant red sunburst on the Tigers' tails have become symbolic of the revived 'Sundowners' tradition, though it contrasts with the two-tone grey tactical paint scheme. In 2007 'Bandit 101' (an ex-Swiss Air Force aircraft) bore the name of the unit's commanding officer, Cdr Rod 'Tool' Dewalt.

27

F-5N 761557/AF 106 of VFC-111, NAS Key West, Florida, 2007

With 15 or more ex-Swiss F-5Ns on strength in 2009, VFC-111 is America's largest operator of Tiger IIs. The unit also has a two-seat F-5F called 'Frankentiger' in its ranks, this aircraft being comprised of the front of a US Navy F-5F and the rear fuselage and wings of a former Swiss F-5E. A variety of camouflage schemes are applied to the squadron's adversaries, representing many of the tactical colours worn by potential threat aircraft that might be encountered anywhere in the world. The desert shades on this aeroplane involve brown, beige and light sand, with the sunburst limited to the rudder only. Other aircraft have shades of blue. The name on the canopy rail is Lt Matthew 'Rub' Morgan.

Back cover

F-14A BuNo 160920/NL 200, flown by Capt S H Hlavka, USS *Kitty Hawk* (CV-63), Autumn 1994

VF-111's last deployment was made in *Kitty Hawk* between June and December 1994, covering the Western Pacific and Indian Ocean. It was also the final cruise of CVW-15, under Capt Stanford H Hlavka, who assumed command shortly before deploying. The 'Sundowners'' CAG bird was typically known as 'The Buick', reflecting the tradition of the senior officer having use of the squadron limousine at NAS Miramar. At one point the name on the jet's RIO canopy rail was AMH1 (AW) C Silvestre, who was probably the squadron's 'Sailor of the Year'. Hlavka led the air wing through the deployment and presided over the disestablishment ceremony in February 1995. BuNo 160920 was initially delivered to VF-213 in January 1980, and served with VF-211, VF-213 again and VF-154 prior to reaching VF-111. Transferred to VF-211 after the 'Sundowners'' disestablishment, the fighter was passed on to VF-41 and eventually struck off charge in February 1999.

Badge 1

'Sundowner' was a term from the age of sail, alluding to a hard-working sailor or captain who toiled until the day was done. In World War 2 the term had obvious Pacific Theatre implications, as VF-11's primary duty was downing Japanese 'suns'.

Badge 2

When VF-111 entered the supersonic age with the arrival of the F8U Crusader in 1961, the 'Sundowners' wanted a special emblem to mark the occasion. A contest was held to determine the squadron mascot, and some sailors in the maintenance department conceived the vaguely oriental stick figure called 'Omar'. He was an immediate sensation, adorning squadron spaces, aircraft and other squadrons' equipment. In one instance 'Omar' appeared on a banner leading the mascots of other squadrons in USS *Kitty Hawk's* CVW-11! He was a part of 'Sundowner' lore until the squadron stood down in 1995, and today remains 'active' with VFC-111.

ACKNOWLEDGEMENTS

The author and publisher acknowledge the invaluable help of the following 'Sundowners', both living and deceased – Rear Adm James B Best, Cdr Robert E Clements, Freeman Darcy, Capt Jerry Dempsey, Cdr Charles G Dimon, Rear Adm Eugene G Fairfax, Robert N Flath, Cdr William C Freckleton, Jr, Rear Adm George M Furlong, Tom Garrett, Cdr Vernon E Graham, Terry H Holberton, Adm James L Holloway III, John Jinks, Rear Adm William N Leonard, Jason Lowrey, Cdr W E Markley, Dave Matheny, Cdr W Robert Maxwell, Cdr H Blake Moranville, Cdr R R Powell, Rear Adm R Emmett Riera, Capt Raymond P Rose, Alex Rucker, Robert J Saggau, Capt Jimmie E Savage, Capt Richard W Schaffert, Cdr Charles R Stimpson, Capt James S Swope, Cdr Tom Twomey, Todd Vieregg, C V Wesley and Adm Ronald J Zlatoper. Extra-special thanks to Kermit 'Tim' Enander.

Thank you also to the following contributors – MCC Jason Chudy, Jini Fairfax, Dewey Ferrell, Caleb Hastings, Richard M Hill, Cdr Jan Jacobs, Rich Leonard, George Mellinger, Lt Cdr Rick Morgan, Mike O'Connor, Walt Quist, José 'Fuji' Ramos, Scott Ramsey, Doug Slowiak, Mike Weeks, Steve Wells, Bill Wright, Capt Todd Zecchin and, of course, Henk 'Omar' van der Lugt and Cdr Doug Siegfried of the Tailhook Association.

BIBLIOGRAPHY

BONIFACE, ROGER, *MiG Pilots Over North Vietnam, 1965-1975*, Hikoki Publications, 2008

FISCHER, COL HAROLD E, RET, *Red Devils on the 38th Parallel* (originally by A A German), Privately published, 2000

FOSTER, WYNN F, *Fire on the Hangar Deck - Ordeal of the Oriskany*, Naval Institute Press, Annapolis, MD, 2001

O'CONNOR, MICHAEL, *MiG Killers of Yankee Station*, New Past Press, Friendship, WI, 2003

TILLMAN, BARRETT, *Sun Downers - VF-11 in World War II*, Phalanx, St Paul, MN, 1993

TILLMAN, BARRETT, 'Korean War Carrier Aviation Review', *The Hook*, Summer 1989

US NAVY, 'Monthly Allowance and Location of Aircraft', 1942-45

Korean War cruise reports of USS *Philippine Sea, Valley Forge, Boxer* and *Lake Champlain*, 1950-53, and Carrier Air Group 11 and Air Task Group 1, 1950-53

WETTERHAHN, RALPH, 'Nguyen Van Bay and the Aces From the North', Air & Space Magazine, November 2000

WEB SITES

ARC Air Discussion Forums:
http://www.arcforums.com/forums/air/index.php?showtopic=133818&st=0

Combat SAR Operations:
http://raunchyredskins.us/Operations/Combat%20SAR.htm

Project Get Out and Walk:
http://www.ejection-history.org.uk/

Ramos Aviation Photography:
http://www.aero-cafe.com/ramosaviation/ramosaviation.html

INDEX